Down MAPLE LANE

Down MAPLE LANE

A Place to Call Home in the Upper Hudson Valley

Elinor Mettler

The History Press

Published by The History Press
Charleston, SC 29403
www.historypress.net

First published 2010

Manufactured in the United States

ISBN 978.1.60949.028.7

Library of Congress Cataloging-in-Publication Data

Mettler, Elinor.
Down Maple Lane : a place to call home in the upper Hudson Valley / Elinor Mettler.
p. cm.
Articles originally published in the Indpendent newspaper in Hillsdale, N.Y.
ISBN 978-1-60949-028-7
1. Columbia County (N.Y.)--History--Anecdotes. 2. Columbia County (N.Y.)--Social life and customs--Anecdotes. 3. Columbia County (N.Y.)--Biography--Anecdotes. 4. Mettler, Elinor. I. Title.
F127.C8M47 2010
974.7'39--dc22
2010034789

Notice: The information in this book is true and complete to the best of our knowledge. It is offered without guarantee on the part of the author or The History Press. The author and The History Press disclaim all liability in connection with the use of this book.

Contents

Preface

Down Maple Lane: A Place to Call Home in the Upper Hudson Valley is a collection of essays about the life and times of a rural area of New York State bordering Massachusetts toward the close of the twentieth century. Roeliff Jansen was an early settler and when the one-room schoolhouse closed, his name was given to the new central school, fondly called Roe Jan. That name covered the five towns composing that district.

"Down Maple Lane" began as a column for a local publication and continued for many years in the *Independent*, a weekly newspaper I published for the community. Several members of my family worked for the paper and have assisted in the creation of this book. Unless noted, all photos are courtesy of the author and the collection of the Roeliff Jansen Historical Society.

My husband, Dr. John Mettler, a veterinarian and author of three books, also contributed to the paper, and it is in his memory that this book is dedicated.

CHAPTER 1
SMALL TOWN

A PLACE WHERE LIVES TOUCH

February 14, 1980

In the city fire sirens are heard frequently; police and ambulance sirens seem to wail endlessly through the night. But from whence comes the call for help that is answered by its shrill cries, dying as it fades into the darkness, is unknown to most of those who hear it. Only if there is trouble on your own block—a fire, accident or sudden illness—or a very short distance down the street, do you know who is in need of emergency help.

Here in the country, in the small town, it's different. While we live much farther apart in distance than those hundreds of families who may fill a city block, our neighborhood ties are closer. We know each other; we are neighbors, friends and relatives—our lives touch, and they are often intertwined. And those who rush to the scene of an emergency to give assistance are also neighbors, friends and relatives.

The person who meets with injury—and perhaps death—is not a stranger, but our brother, father or friend. When the local volunteer firemen and rescue squad, along with police, reporters and clergy, hurry to the scene of an accident, there is always the possibility that the victim is someone they know, which is a situation that would be most unreal in a larger town or city. It is not easy to stand by—unable to change anything and only able to offer a silent prayer when it is your neighbor or the child of your friend who is beyond any human assistance.

The mountains and farms of Copake Falls.

On the other hand, there is something very special about living—yes, and even dying—among friends. There is perhaps some comfort in the fact that, in this community, no one needs to meet the final moment friendless and among strangers any more than anyone needs to live here alone among strangers. It is a place of friendship and of people who give of themselves to help others.

WHERE—AND WHAT—IS "ROE JAN"?

February 21, 1974

The title "Roe Jan area" is often confusing to those who do not live within its bounds. Where is it, they wonder? Or, even before wondering where, they will ask, what is it?

The Roeliff Jansen area is a unique type of community. There is nothing confusing to people when they hear a place called Plainville or Longview. Such names obviously denote towns—very likely small towns—and Small Town, USA, is easily recognized.

But this community known as Roe Jan is something entirely different. On one hand it is a community consisting of three sizable townships: Hillsdale,

Roeliff Jansen Central School, known as Roe Jan, which is now closed, became the center of three towns bearing its name.

Copake and Ancram. On the other, it is one community comprised of several small hamlets, almost too small to be called villages and certainly none large enough to rate the title of a town.

What makes these assorted places hang together? Originally these townships and their hamlets were brought together by a common school district that was formed in 1931. Although this district became part of a much larger one in 1969, the sense of community has persisted and spread even to the newcomers in our area.

Thus, we do not have a Hillsdale Lions Club, Copake Chamber of Commerce or Ancram Community Activities League. The name Roeliff Jansen—or Roe Jan, in brief—has spread from its original use as a name for the school and is the label of anything else that embraces the entire area.

Where did the name come from? We can proudly refer you to our new column on local history that begins in this issue, where you will find your answer. But even after learning what Roeliff Jansen really was, we might still ask the question of who is Roe Jan?

For although we know where it is and what it is (a countryside of rolling hills, gentle mountains, clear streams, "orebeds" and lakes and pleasant hamlets amid fine farmland), the answer to who it is—is people. It is people who cheerfully donate their time as well as a pint of blood for the bloodmobile on Tuesdays. It is the people who care enough about the area to strive to preserve its heritage by banding together in a historical society. It is the people of the churches who worship together weekly and join their neighbors in ecumenical services such as the World Day of Prayer. It is farmers who preserve the open space and rural atmosphere while turning out an abundance of our finest staple: milk. It is the youngsters who are learning useful new skills in their 4-H clubs. It is all those who contribute each in his own way to the good quality of life in the Roe Jan community.

Working on this week's story about Edna St. Vincent Millay provided a particularly memorable day in the nearby hills of Austerlitz. After visiting at Steepletop with the poet's sister, Norma Millay Ellis, we went on touring skis, with her permission, deep into the woods to the place where the poet, her husband and mother have all been laid to rest. There will be many beautiful and remote spots we shall be able to reach on our new skis. But this first trek into the forest at Steepletop, through a shining grove of white birches to this secluded place of rest, will always remain a cherished memory in our hearts.

Roe Jan, then, is more than just a place. It is also people, beauty and countless wonderful happenings like this.

After All, It Is Home

March 13, 1975

When I decided to begin in the *Independent*—a series of portraits of all of our villages that together compose the Roe Jan community—I actually had no plan for any order. Nor did I have any idea of giving any village preference of treatment, placement or time of publication. I had been seeing the assorted sights of our villages for a long time in my travels and kept promising myself that someday I would collect these pictures and publish them for all to enjoy.

Finally the time came; the collection was in progress, and the first portrait was scheduled for this week. There's no particular reason why Copake Falls made it first—it was pure chance. But then again, it seems quite appropriate because, after all, it is home.

Copake Falls has been home for nearly twenty-eight consecutive years and was more or less home for a long time before that. Summers were spent here in the house seen in the background of one of the photographs in today's portrait. And, a long trek though it was, nearly every weekend

Our first little home in the village of Copake Falls.

for the rest of the year, the family found itself at its Copake Falls home. Then for two winters we stayed and went to school here. Perhaps it was because the family's everyday home changed from time to time while Copake Falls remained constant—this was the more permanent place called "home."

One generally goes back home for one's marriage, so it was in Copake Falls that the wedding took place on a summer's day in the little old church that's no longer here. And it was here that we settled into our first home and later built the home to fit the family (more or less)—the home I love so dearly and never see enough of.

I don't know just what the population of Copake Falls is now, but not many years ago we sat out in our backyard one day and not only counted but actually named off all—or almost all—of its inhabitants. When our children who made the count went away from home, they delighted in this tiny town rather than be ashamed to admit that they came from such a place. It's not everyone who can name nearly all the people in the place where they live! And I'm sure the very idea boggled the minds of metropolitan types they'd tell about our little hometown.

A few weeks ago we quoted Frank Stang, who said that people who go all over the world come back and say it is best here. We've been far away and have seen some wonderful sights. But we agree that that judgment suits our whole Roe Jan area and, for us, this particular little village that is nestled close to the mountains. I have chosen it, like many others, over the city and suburban life we left behind. And I never tire of looking out our windows at those mountains, particularly in the pink afterglow of the sunset.

There are many things we could probably tell about our village, and we'll have to admit it isn't the most perfect of villages, by any means. But we're happy here. It's been a good place for us to live and our family to grow up.

While I personally find much interest in every one of our local villages, there's one thing special about the village portrayed in our centerfold today. It was written in cross-stitch on a sampler that hung in our old house there long ago: travel east, travel west, after all home is best.

Three Cheers—and More!

June 16, 1983

It was a perfect June afternoon. People gathered in the shade of a big old maple and stood, talking quietly in front of the newly painted building with red geraniums blooming brightly around its front steps. The American flag flew from its porch, and at two o'clock, conversation stopped and everyone recited the Pledge of Allegiance and then moved indoors to fill the seats in front of the dais and the old benches lining the walls. Wild phlox in an old crock in front of the railing provided simple decoration. Sun shone in the narrow-arched windows.

Then the program began. A prayer was recited and an inspiring song was sung. Words of appreciation were voiced by speakers, along with the expressions of the joy that comes with seeing a dream realized. After another song by the choir, the entire assembly rose to its feet to join in on a heartfelt chorus of *God Bless America.*

After the program was over and the exhibits were seen, people came out under the shade tree again for a cup of punch and a lovely selection of cookies from a table decorated in the patriotic colors of the approaching Flag Day. People stood around a long time, chatting and agreeing that it had been a lovely occasion and, indeed, a perfect day, seeming loath to break the spell.

It was our town, celebrating a very special occasion in a plain, old-fashioned way, the dedication of the Old Copake Falls Church as a historic public building.

Its restoration and preservation had been but a dream at one time; now, it was a dream that really came true.

This Methodist church building became a historical society museum.

In a short time, the town turned the building over to the Roeliff Jansen Historical Society for it to become a museum of local history. The society maintains it as a repository for its collection of historic items and information and mounts special exhibits every summer.

Everyone Needs a Hometown

November 26, 2009

For some people it's the place where they were born and maybe never left. For many it's the place to go back to, maybe for school or family reunions. Maybe it's for retirement, or maybe it's just because you're becoming weary

Once a store, this building now holds the post office.

of spending every day in a place where no one knows you or takes the trouble to find out who you are; a place where you can go about your business day after day without exchanging a friendly word with anyone—not the clerk in a store, not the cop on the beat and not the people who live in the next apartment. The word "hometown" begins to sound really good.

The hometown you return to—or choose to move to—is a welcoming place. There's the old story about the woman behind the counter at the general store (presupermarkets) who smiled as she packed your things and said, "Oh, you're the people living in the old Preston place." What was your first reaction to this? Did you shudder as you wondered, how does she know me or how come she knows where I live? Or had you already managed to shed your city ways, including a fear of someone knowing all about you? What was your reaction to her openness: fear or delight? Was she being nosey—or friendly and welcoming? Experience will tell you that it's the latter; it was just a matter of being friendly and interested in neighbors.

You may be used to having your mail drop through a slot in the front door or appear in one of many boxes lined up in the entrance hall of your apartment.

Whether you live in a village or on an RFD (previously known as Rural Free Delivery), you might find that a daily trip to the village post office is a delightful way of starting a country day. Why? It's because you will meet people there. Take the time to make introductions and have a visit. In retirement, my husband could take longer to go to the post office than anyone. That was because, as our postmaster said, he talked to everyone: the most important people in town and the new immigrants to our area who worked on the farms.

Things change, of course, even in small towns, as population increases. It wasn't so long ago that when my mother happened to make a mistake dialing a phone number she realized she had inadvertently reached someone she knew and they had a delightful chat before hanging up. And it wasn't unusual to have someone stop their car in the middle of the village street you were crossing to catch up on the news with you.

One thing that is growing bigger lately is a town meeting of any kind. When Copake's Comprehensive Planning Committee announced a meeting to be held on a recent Saturday morning, a time when most people want to work on their yard, play golf, or not do much of anything, the Town Hall was packed. It was simply the place to be, at least for all those people who really care about their old or newly acquired hometown. They could have written a lengthy column about what they like about their town; from the scenery to the people and back, they told it all. And they had lots of ideas about things that might be added to make life even better in their town.

Over the years this column has covered that subject often and in a variety of ways. What it all adds up to is that we hometown folks, old or new, really care about our special place, and are willing to do what each of us can to make it even better. It might even become the kind of place our children, as they grow up and explore the rest of the world, will someday want to come home to.

The Good Life

March 28, 1976

Those of us who have lived in the city (and that includes the very densely populated suburbs) or who live there all week, escaping to the country only on weekends, know that there are many reasons why we love the country and prefer living here. But if there is one particular reason why country life is preferable, what is it?

Until recently a busy dairy farm area, there were more beef cows than traffic on the main highway.

During an interview last week, an émigré from Long Island attempted to explain what she likes better about her life here. "It's so relaxing," she said, which we both found laughable because we were talking in a dairy barn at chore time, occurring with somewhat grim regularity every twelve hours. It's hardly what you'd call "relaxing."

Trying again to define the pleasing difference between the old life there and the new life here, she said "Long Island is so congested." Leaving there and driving home, past numerous such farms on a town road and several miles along a county road, I passed one car and only two or three more on a couple of miles of state highway. Without realizing the significance of my train of thought, I found myself thinking about how amazing this would be to some friends we visited on Long Island a few weeks ago after attending the Press Association Convention in a cluttered, congested and unlovely section. Many years earlier, one of our friends living in that area remarked that he thought of Copake Falls every time he tried to make a left turn into traffic a few blocks from his home, something the residents of Maple Lane do with ease every morning.

Suddenly it was clear what this fairly new resident of the Roe Jan area felt and was trying to express. The fact that the area is so uncongested is what gives her the feeling that life is relaxed, even though most of us find little free time for real relaxation. We are just as busy as our city cousins and, in some cases, busier. But even our work is easier to accomplish because we don't have to battle traffic to get to it every day. The farmer has a short and solitary walk to his barn; the tradesman has a brief drive to his shop; and even those who commute as far a distance as suburbanites—perhaps an hour—do so on uncrowded highways. Someone once admitted to a certain pleasure derived from listening on the car radio to helicopter reports on traffic tie-ups on the Long Island Expressway while breezing along Route 22 each morning on the way to work.

Not only do we avoid automobile traffic, but we are not crushed by large segments of the human race in crowded subway cars and elevators before we reach our desks each morning. If we go out to lunch, we may even be able to go back to our own kitchen for it. But wherever we take that midday break, we are not apt to have someone breathing down our necks, waiting to grab our seats the minute we take the last bite of our lunch.

Nor is it a hassle to get back home in the evening. With the exception of the kids on the school bus, we don't have to share mass transit with anyone, and it usually doesn't take too long to get there. With only one traffic light within the whole Roe Jan area, there's little chance of getting slowed down by hitting all the red lights.

With the lack of congestion due, of course, to the low population, the country is so much quieter. When one can walk up the road and hear the *plink-plink* of the maple sap dropping into the buckets, that's quiet! And when the only visible sign of "rush hour" is the next group of cows crowding through the door to the milking parlor, that's the good life!

CHAPTER 2
COUNTRY LIFE

ONE-ROOM SCHOOL DAYS

August 27, 2009

Marguerite Prior couldn't have been more than seventeen or eighteen years old when she began to teach the children of North Hillsdale with all eight grades in a one-room school. She appears in a photograph of the small group of graduates of the Hillsdale High School, Class of 1916. She could have gone for a year or more of training at a "normal school," but very likely she just began to teach at that young age.

She was paid twenty-six dollars a week, earning a raise of one dollar more each year at Hillsdale District Ten in the hamlet of North Hillsdale. The schoolhouse was located between the general store and the Methodist church. She was followed there by a woman known as Hattie B. Dean, who lived with her husband in a house near the school. By then the salary rose to thirty dollars a week with two weeks' vacation.

The trustees were people who lived within that small neighborhood. Schools were within walking distance for the children. Their locations appear on 1873 maps of the towns, which also list the names of the homeowners. The trustees' report to the New York State Department of Education in 1931 shows a student body of eleven girls and seven boys of a variety of ages and grades in the school.

The report notes that Article Twenty-seven of the Education Law of 1910 required a school to have an American flag and the pupils to be taught its correct use and display. Article Twenty-six required the teaching

The young teacher, *left*, and her pupils in the North Hillsdale one-room school.

This schoolhouse served the children of Copake Falls until the central school opened in the early 1930s.

of physiology and hygiene. The students were also taught the humane treatment of birds and animals. In the eighth grade, the youngsters were to study the history and meaning of the U.S. Constitution. By the age of eight, they received instruction on patriotism and citizenship.

The report asked how many trees had been planted on school grounds and whether Arbor Day was properly observed. And there were the required "privies or water closets" available to the children, which were properly inspected at the little school.

At the time of the 1911 report, District Ten had two students who had completed eight grades. A local man was paid $1.60 per day to drive them to Hillsdale for high school. Before the Roeliff Jansen building opened in 1932, students attended classes at the Mount Washington House (hotel). At least one of them liked to tell his children that he went to school in the bar room there.

Getting back to Miss Prior, her longevity as a teacher was quite remarkable. While she had taught this gentleman in about 1930 at District Ten, she also taught the fifth of his six children in third grade at the Roe Jan school in about 1965, some thirty years later. And she was not only teaching early in her long career, along with making sure the flag was properly displayed, that animals were treated humanely and that Arbor Day was observed, but she was also keeping a close eye on the condition of the outdoor privies.

Those Dear Old Golden School Days

June 19, 1980

It is graduation time again. For the past few weeks, the pages of the *Independent* have been filled with news of young people graduating from college, and this week it's time for high school graduation and eighth-grade exercises. It's an exciting time for the graduates, who look forward to something new and the next step in life—an adventure, whether high school or college, the service or a new job.

But for parents, it's a time tinged with sadness, for the child who is graduating is taking a step away from the shelter of home. Never again can that childhood of the eighth-grader or the youth of high school days be recaptured. Nor can our own.

Suddenly—surprisingly—as these words are written, the Boston Pops, which is playing on public radio, swings into an encore. It is a Glenn Miller arrangement of "Moonlight Serenade," and memories of happy high school days come flooding back: the friendships, the fun, the classmates, the dances, plays, concerts, parties, games, student election campaigns, pep rallies and hours spent with pals over a five-cent Coke. All of it was over too soon, and it fades into dim memory, except when awakened by a song.

It's not only in recent times that boys left the shelter of home and high school to go to war. They went then, too, and some never returned. Wartime was a way of life for those of us who were young then. There wasn't the usual fun of college life to look forward to. The boys went off to war, and girls went, too, or were left at home to work or go to college, spending the next few growing years as women who were learning to live in a world without men. Letters and all too brief furloughs were precious, and the fun of school days were a mere memory all too soon in our young lives. But perhaps the fact that those high school days were our last happy school days makes the memory of them all the more precious.

At least at this moment in time, our children are not threatened as seventeen- and eighteen-year-olds were then and were again by two more wars. As these Classes of 1980 conclude their high school days, we hope they have been happy ones to look back on—to be brought vividly alive again at some far-off future time at the sound of a haunting refrain by one of today's popular bands or singers. And we pray that they will be able to live in a future of peace, learning, hopefully, how to keep that peace better than we did.

Memories of a Landmark

March 21, 1974

In all of the Roe Jan area, Ancram is the only place left where you can pick up the morning mail and your groceries under the same roof. And even that location was recently changed to different quarters.

Many years ago, the post office was often located within a general store, and this was the case in many places—in fact, probably all the villages—of the area. The one I remember best is John Keating's store in Copake Falls. It stood at the foot of a hilly spot on the road now called Route 344, just past the old Tri-State Inn. Its proper, more elegant name was Keating's New York Store.

Going to the post office at Keating's (and as children, we were sent often) provided a glimpse into the past. Even in those days, the business had

Keating's store housed the Copake Falls post office.

declined. Village people didn't do much trading there, and the canned goods on the shelves—a fancy brand—were gathering dust. But the atmosphere was one that many young storekeepers are trying to duplicate today.

The post office was at the front on your right as you entered. As I recall there was penny candy in the case to the left of the post office counter. There were no keys or combinations to the mail boxes. You asked the postmaster or his clerk, Katherine Melius, for your mail at the counter beside the boxes, on which stood a white china roller in its own receptacle of water for dampening stamps. I don't know why post offices don't have these today instead of sponges or unsanitary licking. A child could be amused by the roller while waiting for the mail to be sorted, and you could look up behind the counter to see the boxes of high-button shoes, still there on the shelves.

In the rear of the store was the grocery counter, and there were shelves of canned goods in the center. But the best place of all was the dry-goods counter at the front of the store on the left. In front of it were two or three little stools where ladies once sat while selecting goods for a dress or whatever they needed to make for the family or household. You could sit on those little stools, which were permanently connected to the floor, and spin around to your heart's content while waiting for your family's letters.

Then there was the front porch of the store with a bench for waiting. Or, since it was high enough above the road, you could sit on the edge and swing your feet until the mail carrier brought the mail bags from the railroad station in a small truck. You could watch him putting the bags in the back of the truck as the taxis picking up rail passengers pulled away from the station.

Since the mail came to the area by train in those "good old days" of the three-cent stamp, it arrived several times a day. Now it seems remarkable that you could sit on the porch reading a letter mailed to you from New York that very day. Or if your letter was put on the evening train down, the recipient in New York could have it first thing in the morning.

The rural route from Copake Falls to Mount Washington, Massachusetts, that still exists today was more popular among the mountain residents at that time, for they could have groceries delivered with the mail at the same time. They were, therefore, Keating's best and, in the end, perhaps only customers.

But everything has changed, and Keating's New York Store is no more. It burned down one night many years ago, and the story was that John Keating, nephew of previous owner Thomas Keating, lost everything, including books and records. He died not long afterward.

We lived many summers and a few winters on Miles Road in those days, and we had a path that went through the field, just between the houses from our road to a point just below the post office, that was well used. Although active as the location of the post office, Keating's New York Store was a dying business even then. It would have been fun to have seen it in its heyday and to have sat on those little stools while our mother selected yard goods for our Sunday dresses.

THE CHURCH SUPPER: A COMMUNITY INSTITUTION

November 1, 1973

It is a trite but true cliché that nothing stays the same, although that can be challenged by another popular belief that things never really change. However, anyone who has ever tried to go back home after many years absence usually finds that the old hometown is scarcely as one remembers it. The picture in one's mind of the hometown as it was way back when proves to be merely a memory. There are new buildings changing the scene, and lots of new faces among the population—perhaps a whole new generation. With new people come new ideas and new activities in town.

The town supervisor, *left*, mashes potatoes for the church supper.

And yet there are some things that continue on forever, it seems, carried from one generation to another and enjoyed as much by the newcomers in town as the old-timers. One such local phenomenon is the "church supper."

We use the quotes because while the actual church suppers seem to have been going on the longest, other organizations have recognized a good thing when they see it and gotten into the act. Scouts (and their parents) put on spaghetti suppers, the Lions and churches have had chicken barbecues, the Granges have always put on a variety of suppers and there have been smorgasbords at the school to benefit the senior class—just to mention a few. The pancake breakfasts the Lions put on for the student exchange fund and Boy Scouts have become something of an institution in just a few years, and so have the pancake and sausage supper the Copake Fire no. 2 Auxiliary serves each year on the first night of deer season, giving the hunters not only a good hot meal after a day in the woods but also a gathering place to swap yarns of the day's conquests or the one that got away.

But of all the barbecues, smorgasbords, ham, roast beef or pancake suppers, nothing surpasses the good old-fashioned turkey supper (synonymous with church supper) cooked and served by several churches in the Roe Jan area every fall. Some of them have been going on for so many years that no one really remembers just when they began. Usually the same folks have been cooking, serving and washing up for years and have their jobs down to a science. The ticket price is naturally higher than it used to be, but it's still a bargain for the good quality and great quantity of the food.

Upon entering the hall and finding a place to sit at the long tables, one is greeted by the delicious aromas emanating from the busy kitchen. Rolls and butter are on the tables, along with cranberries and coleslaw. Within a few minutes, the hot food starts coming, served by the younger women and teenage girls of the congregation. In rapid succession, steaming bowls of mashed potatoes, mashed turnips, stuffing and gravy, and finally a platter heaped with white and dark meat turkey appear. The dishes are handed around to one another until plates are full and conversation lags. As soon as a serving dish looks half empty an attentive waitress snatches it up and returns with a brimming refill. In due time, most everyone at the table takes a second helping, and a few really serious eaters probably get thirds. The platters are never completely empty, and one could eat until bursting, as the supply seems unlimited.

Without a noticeable lull, it gets to be dessert time. Dishes are cleared away ("keep your fork"), and a choice of pies are announced, generally apple, mince and pumpkin, traditional to the season. Meanwhile, scalding pitchers of coffee have filled the big white cups, as well as milk for the kids and others who prefer it.

Suddenly the room becomes very noisy, and it's obvious that people have finished eating and have begun to visit with their neighbors. People who may not have seen each other for months meet at the annual supper. In fact, they may have met last at the supper the previous year. Politicians running for office always used to travel the turkey-supper circuit in the month before Election Day, as it was the best way to meet a lot of people and shake a lot of hands. It's doubtful they could stand the sight of turkey by the time the people went to the polls.

Diners at the church supper can't linger too long after polishing off their pie with its chunk of cheddar, for there's another supper crowd gathering to come in and take their places. And so it starts all over again—three times in all—until the last ticket holder is replete. Then, at last, the zealous workers get their turn to sit down and pitch into their own good, wholesome cooking and relax a bit before finishing off the last of the cleaning job. And they probably start talking about plans for next year's annual church supper.

The Old Party Line

July 19, 1979

It used to hang on the wall in the kitchen in our country house: a big, varnished, wooden box of rectangular shape with bells at the top, a black mouthpiece protruding at about center above a slanted shelf, the black earpiece hanging at one side and a little handle for ringing up the contraption on the other side. This was our telephone, the kind everyone around here used to have in the not-so-distant past.

An early telephone on which one rang up the operator and got personal service.

It might sound like a formidable machine, difficult to work, but it wasn't. You didn't even have to dial it to make a call! You just "rang up" the operator with the little handle and gave her the numbers, and she did all the rest. In fact, you very often could skip the number by just mentioning the name of the friend, relative, storekeeper or doctor you wanted to talk to. The operators for the old Copake Telephone Company certainly didn't need you to tell them the numbers—they knew them all. Nor did you have to wait for a busy signal to find out your sister wasn't home. Clarissa, or the other operators, already knew she'd gone out and probably where she'd gone. If anyone ever really had their finger on the "pulse of the community," it was these women.

The present-day telephone company tells us it will have an answering service available in the not-too-distant future, and in the meantime it has recording devices for those who need someone—or something—to take their calls. Well, those things certainly weren't needed in the old days, not with those operators on the job. "Doc" Bowerhan and several others had an efficient "answering service" long before anyone ever heard of such a thing. The local operators knew his whereabouts at all times and could probably tell today's dispatchers a few tales!

There used to be a lot of houses on each party line, each with its own ring. There could be two, three, four, five or six short rings, one long and two short, one long and three short, etc., and it rang on every instrument on the line. In every house, every ring was heard, though, of course, you only picked up the receiver for your own ring—or did you? Listening in on the party line was a fact of country life and a simple way for the old-time reporter to gather her "personals" for the week's column.

That great giant of a phone finally was replaced by a "French" phone, but not before it brought a soldier's call all the way from Hawaii during the winding down of World War II. One had to hope not too many receivers went up during that call.

When we were married and moved permanently to Copake Falls just thirty-two years ago today, the phone installed in our first home was the upright style with the receiver hanging on the side, requiring two hands to use, which was not the quickest thing to grab when an emergency call came in the night. Now there's one of these, although somewhat fancier, on display at the new office of the Taconic Telephone Corp. (the very expanded outgrowth of the Copake Company), along with the Mickey Mouse phone, the flip phone, the replica of the real French phone and others. Now we're offered all sorts of new options, like having calls automatically transferred (Clarissa used to do that automatically if we went visiting), and push buttons that are quicker than dialing.

But even though there are some really pleasant and helpful people on the other end, on the occasions when you dial *0* for assistance, nothing will ever be the same as hearing my mother ring up the old phone, start to give a number and then interrupt to say something like Fibber McGee's "That you Myrt?" and get into a conversation with the friendly hometown operator before going ahead with her call.

A Country House

August 4, 1977

The photo with this section brings back lots of memories. Nowadays, city and suburban people heading to the country for the summer go to "ranch" houses, split-levels, A-frames and other contemporary dwellings. Any kind of house in the country is a welcome change, especially in summer, but the old-fashioned country house—like the one photographed—is very special because it's the kind many of us came to for childhood summers.

The old-fashioned country house is white with shutters. It has an old-fashioned kitchen with a kitchen table—no chrome, mind you—the drop-leaf kind that can be extended with extra leaves and probably has had several coats of paint applied. There may be a combination wood/gas stove where the big, black, wood cookstove once stood.

There's a bedroom up under the eaves where you have to duck your head when you sit up in bed. There are round places in the ceiling where stovepipes used to go through, and an open grillwork register that lets the heat go through to a chilly upstairs bedroom. These openings are special fun for kids who want to see and hear what's going on downstairs after they've been sent to bed. They also offer an opportunity for tricks, such as running a nearly invisible thread down to a pen sitting on a table below the opening; that pen can suddenly be whisked up out of reach when an unsuspecting adult is urged to pick it up.

The stairway is narrow—if it's the original one—and there may be back stairs to the backroom where the hired hand slept above the "summer kitchen."

Houses like these always have porches with rockers, where kids can read lots of books all summer, and adults can rock and talk far into the warm summer evenings. It also has swings: rope swings in the shade trees, and painted garden swings that seat four adults for conversation or provide kids

An example of the typical country house with flower boxes and rockers on the porch for summer relaxation.

with a vehicle that can be a train, a car, a plane—and now probably an imaginary spaceship.

Such a house may also still boast an outhouse out back, with the inside walls papered with something flowery as a pattern or, better still, the pages of an old book of flowery poems (like a long-remembered one—illustrated—about Mr. and Mrs. Cockatoo). It will also have a toolshed and even a barn that makes a wonderful playhouse or clubhouse for youngsters lucky enough to spend their summers at a country house like this.

These houses have old-fashioned gardens with the kind of flowers that come up year after year, and they have outdoor pumps or bucket wells where the water is best for a cool drink on a hot day.

As older houses are remodeled or changed to become year-round homes, the old-fashioned "house in the country" is becoming a rarity. Hopefully it will not become extinct.

Something Is Missing

May 25, 1978

We were talking the other day about the forthcoming Northeast Dairy Day that will be celebrated in Copake on June 27. To nonfarmers, the change to bulk handling of milk on the farm may not seem like a very earthshaking event. But it revolutionized dairy farming and the many kinds of agribusiness that serve it.

It also made vast differences in a dairy farmer's way of life: the way he milks his cows, the way he feeds them, the kind of equipment he uses and so on. Perhaps a more subtle change is the way in which a farmer's day is affected. He still gets up at a terrible hour of the morning to begin milking, even with all the automation. But when morning milking is done, he goes to the house for breakfast, works on his books and then returns to barn chores or field work. The milk is picked up; the feed is delivered; and the farmer never has to leave the place. Is it an improvement? Well…

In the old days, a farmer drove to the milk plant every morning with his cans of milk. Then he went to the feed and general stores, where he picked up a few things on the shopping list given to him by his wife. But not only did he have these chores and errands to do in town every morning, he also had the opportunity to fraternize with fellow farmers, visit with townspeople, "chew the rag" a bit and experience community. Now that milk is picked up, feed is delivered and the farmer's wife has plenty on hand in the freezer, these daily opportunities for communication have been lost.

And hasn't this happened to people in all walks of life? The many conveniences, the many ways we have become self-sufficient, have also deprived us—unless we go to the Laundromat—of seeing people every day while about the simple process of everyday life. Many have replaced the daily visit to the grocery, where one meets neighbors and chats with the storekeeper who knows customers' names, with a weekly or monthly drive to a huge self-service market some distance from home where the cashier—who doesn't look at anyone—is the only human being involved. Banking by mail, ordering by mail and all sorts of "do it yourself" have created a self-sufficient and lonely people.

It takes a lot longer to get the mail, for example, when you walk up the street to the post office and engage in several conversations along the way. But it certainly makes for a more cheerful day, and it's one of the many simple joys of small-town life.

This page: Before the advent of big tank trucks picking up the milk at farms, farmers drove cans of milk each day to a local plant for shipment.

Hurricanes We Have Known

October 3, 1985

It was near deadline last week when my husband called and asked, "Have you written Maple Lane yet…about Budd Tudge running down the road with his raincoat behind him?" He'd been listening to the dire forecasts of Hurricane Gloria on the weather radio and remembered that oft-told tale of our old friend bringing news of the railroad bridge in Copake Falls going out in the 1938 hurricane to which Gloria was being compared. Sure enough, when my brother, sister and I followed him up Miles Road, where my old family home was located, the tracks curved down like a roller coaster.

School was closed because so many bridges went out with the high water, but everyone seemed to be able to get around for sightseeing to view damages. That was before hurricanes had names, but apparently the severity of its surprise attack gave weather service the impetus to start naming and forecasting hurricanes.

In 1955, Diane hit with heavy rain. We awoke to hear our dogs barking and found them up to their necks in water while the debris coming down the Bash Bish was floating past the house. The Maple Lane Bridge had

The 1938 hurricane took out these railroad tracks.

gone out and diverted the raging stream to an old brook bed bordering our property. The water was starting to come up through the cellar floor and very shortly began pouring in the cellar windows, reaching five feet. A little rabbit floating around on a log sought safety on the stairway. What a blessing that when Fred Clark built our new home only a few years earlier, he'd had the wisdom to excavate only five feet for the basement and build it up two feet or our main floor would have been flooded and left covered with silt.

That time the Bash Bish took with it not only a small cottage on Miles Road but one of the big, old miners "cottages" from the state park.

In late June 1973, when the *Independent* was only three issues old, we awoke on a Saturday morning to results of yet another hurricane. That time it was Carol, I think, and she caused a lot of damage near every stream, even those usually a mere trickle. I was in the car from early morning until evening photographing all those places, and later writing the blow-by-blow story:

> *The first call from the Roe Jan area came over the "hot line" to the Columbia County Sheriff's Department Saturday morning around 7:15 and ironically it was from Marge Proper, wife of Under-Sherriff* [sic] *Paul Proper, who alerted the emergency headquarters in the county court house when she and her son discovered a sudden flood heading toward their home from across Dean's field on the opposite side of the road. Her husband had already left the house an hour earlier to investigate a report of water flowing across Route 23 west of Hillsdale. Firemen reached her home within minutes. Just beyond the Proper's home the parking lot of the Copake Theatre looked like a lake and the newly constructed miniature golf course across the road at the Carousel was completely swamped. Up the road on the other side of the overflowing Bash Bish Darlene Hamm saw the water rise to the top step of her cellar stairway and knew it was time to evacuate the children and the older folks.*

That was when the "nearly lost" boys came to stay with us. I'd met them a few days earlier when they got off the New York bus in Copake with their bikes to do some riding and camping. Finding them barefoot in Copake that morning, I learned they'd lost most of their belongings (including shoes) as water flowed down the mountain, and they could very well have lost their lives. We clothed and fed them until the New York bus was able to get through again the following day.

There was another storm whose name I've forgotten that gave us some flooding—water in the cellar at least. The one thing I recall was saving the old rocking chair stored in our cellar. I'd sold it at an IFE flea market several weeks earlier to a New Yorker buying a country home and promised to store it until he got the house. "Save the rocker," I called; then I grabbed the camera and ran.

It doesn't take much to flood certain familiar spots in our area. All we got from Gloria was rain and temporarily high water, with a bit of wind, though nothing to equal our customary last blows.

Few lives were lost, and due to the storm hitting Long Island and Connecticut at low tide, damage was not as great as anticipated. But thousands of people in those areas were without electric power days later, which had a tremendous effect on modern life in urban and suburban areas. Rather than the Monday morning quarterbacking that began immediately among news commentators (Dr. Frank, didn't you overestimate the storm?), the public should be thankful that the weather bureau's tracking system gave them ample time to evacuate or even to just stock up on water, flashlight batteries, etc. Better safe than sorry.

Now, who's next among these now mixed-gender storms (with Henri having slipped by)? Ina, Ida, Imogene?

Old Times, Old Remedies

January 24, 1985

Last week's "Inch of Wind," recalling the experiences and remedies of childhood colds, brought back many memories to us, and, no doubt, to many readers. Who cannot immediately recall the various vapors attendant upon those colds of old?

My mother's cure-all for that common ailment was to plunge the feet of the one whose head was stuffed into a dishpan of scalding water made hotter and more pungent by a healthy dollop of dry mustard. The "hot mustard foot bath" it was called, and what it had to do with congestion in the head and/or chest, I'm still not sure. Perhaps its intense heat and steaming vapors drew some of that misery from the upper portions of one's person. Or maybe the almost painful scalding of the feet simply made one forget about what else had been feeling miserable. After soaking and sniffling for a while, when the foot bath began to cool to lukewarm—become bearable, that is—the feet were hastily wrapped in a thick "Turkish" towel and the patient was bundled off to bed. Perhaps that's where the remedy went into its second stage, as the object was to be very warm and begin to sweat out the cold.

I don't know where my mother got her recipe for this remedy, possibly from the label on a box of Colman's English mustard. The label in the newest box of dry mustard in my cupboard merely suggests using it to flavor various foods. But far in the back of the cupboard is a box of Colman's English that, I think, came from my mother's house. Its label tells nothing of the pungent foot bath, but it does have a recipe for a "Mustard Plaster or Poultice (adults)...Take equal parts of flour and Colman's Mustard and make into a paste with tepid water. Spread on cotton cloth and cover with a second piece. Apply and allow to remain as long as can be borne but not more than 20 minutes. For sensitive skins increase the amount of flour used to four parts flour to one part mustard."

My friend (and typographer) Irene has vivid memories of a mustard plaster her mother applied to the chests of ailing children. It was made with lard mixed with the mustard rather than flour. After it was on the child awhile, it beaded up, she recalls. Irene also remembers a mixture of wintergreen or peppermint oil mixed into a cup of hot water (with a little sugar to sweeten it) for stomach ailments.

We all remember camphorated oil, especially the song that went along with its application to the tune of "John Brown's Body": "John Brown's baby had a cold upon its chest (repeat twice) and they rubbed it with camphorated oil." (Was this an early vintage singing commercial?) This could be accompanied by appropriate gestures, rocking the baby, rubbing the chest, sneezing, etc.

One of the most unusual things Irene remembers is the headache remedy her mother apparently learned from earlier generations: slices of peeled potato were laid into a bandana or other piece of cloth tied around the head so the potatoes laid across the forehead to soothe the aching head.

The pleasures of working one's way through a cold as a youngster are memorable, too. It wasn't a serious illness, just enough, as was said last week, to permit one to stay out of school lounging in bed with books and—not TV in our day—but a bedside radio. That radio kept us company, especially if we had a "working mother," with a different cast of characters every fifteen minutes: *Ma Perkins*, *Stella Dallas*, *Backstage Wife*—soap operas far different, far more innocent in their plots, than the TV soaps of today, with each introduced by its own organ theme and sponsored by products like Oxydol, which seems to have gone the way of the innocent soap opera.

Also on the bedside table, of course, was the orange juice, replaced later by eggnog and, at lunchtime, by my mother's surefire remedy for whatever ailed you: not chicken soup, but rich and delicious "beef tea." My husband recalls that his mom's specialty for her ailing child was always vanilla cornstarch pudding.

We might wonder what such memories our children will have—if not any nostalgia for staying home to be nursed through the common cold, perhaps of the more serious childhood illnesses that predated the vaccines that now prevent them. One of the good memories of those times would have to be the bedside visits of Dr. Bowerhan, warming with his hands the stethoscope he took out of his black bag before placing it on their feverish little bodies.

CHAPTER 3

PEOPLE

A LIFE WELL SPENT

July 24, 1980

Frank Stang died this week after a long, hard struggle with ill health, and the village will be different without him. The gas station he started as a spunky lad of sixteen will still be there on Church Street, as it has been for the past fifty-one years, with members of his family still working the pumps for all the longtime customers, but it won't ever be quite the same again. It's kind of like the end of an era.

Frank was of a generation whose life could be lived within a limited area, something that becomes more and more unusual in these times of great mobility of people. He was born in Copake, went to school there, became a businessman at the tender age of sixteen, married a girl from not too far out of town and raised his children in a house just a few doors up the street from the garage he operated for more than fifty years, swinging down the street to work or puttering along in his old truck to give the bad leg a rest. And on Sunday, he died in his beloved hometown, just up the street from the old stand where he had held forth as a friend, confidant and advisor to so many men and boys for all of those years, and he was laid to rest yesterday in the cemetery just across the street from the garage where he spent all of his adult life.

Yet, although he rarely left the village of Copake—except to run business errands nearby—his influence was felt far and wide by those who had known him. Perhaps they knew him from their own years of growing up (and have

Usually in his work clothes, Frank dresses up for a party in his honor.

moved to far-off places) and by his "summer trade," which returned to him regularly since the 1930s. People remembered him every year with a Christmas card, and they will remember him still, long after he has gone from this place where he belonged.

Frank's life of sixty-seven years was a fairly short span, lived out entirely in one small place, but it was a good life that touched and influenced the lives of many people. And how fine it was that those people—his devoted family and scores of friends—let him know how much they appreciated him during his lifetime. Here was a man who was honored with enthusiastic testimonials not once but twice during his lifetime. "His whole heart is here in the community. There isn't anything he wouldn't do for anybody," one of them once said. Frank's simple explanation of that was, "I love Copake"—and the feeling was mutual.

Up To Budd's

August 16, 1984

Although we can't really call ourselves natives, there are many of us in the Roe Jan community who have lived here so long and have come summers and weekends for so many years before—even since childhood—that we feel like natives; to all outward appearances we are. One among us, who was known for so long by so many that he was an integral part of this place, was Budd Tudge.

Budd and his brother, Ted, came to Copake Falls, as did many others who eventually called it home, as youngsters coming to the Rest, a summer camp for mothers and children operated by the Church of the Heavenly Rest in New York City. He and I talked about doing a story about the Rest for the *Independent* but unfortunately never found the time.

Budd continued to come to Copake Falls as a young man, staying at Carrie Melius's boardinghouse and spending time at the ore bed. Whenever the hurricane and flood of 1938 is recalled, I can picture Budd running down the road to our house, with his navy blue trench coat flying out behind him, calling to us to come quick—the railroad bridge was going down.

At the Waldorf Astoria, he received the training as a chef, for which he was always very proud, following in the footsteps of his father, who'd been a chef at the old Ritz Carlton. He went off to North Africa as a cook, returning when the United States got into World War II. He was drafted and worked at a hospital in the European Theater.

But eventually he came back to this place he loved best and to build a small takeout-type of eating place; he gradually enlarged it to accommodate diners and dinner parties. I remember the day it burned, leaving only the chimney. Budd decided to start all over again there, and the community welcomed him back.

Every small community has its gathering places, and Budd's restaurant was one of them. You couldn't eat there without meeting someone—and more likely several people—you knew, so dinner at Budd's was a social affair. People talked back and forth across the dining room, which perhaps perplexed strangers who had just stopped by, although many transients traveling Route 22 were certainly regulars there.

And of course, a conversation with Budd was always part of having lunch or dinner there. The kitchen door was always open—he didn't want to miss greeting anyone. More often than not, as you were leaving, Budd came out to have a chat. While he certainly loved cooking, seeing his friends—and they were legion—was a big part of his running a restaurant.

When a person dies suddenly, without warning, it is always a terrible shock to those left behind, and when that person is so well-known, the shock waves travel far and wide. That someone, who for so long has been a real part of the community, will be sorely missed. The restaurant will be continued by the family, so it will still be Tudge's. But it won't be quite the same. It won't be going "up to Budd's."

Two Great Gals

November 21, 1974

Two very wonderful women touched my life this day, one young and the other very old. A motto above my desk reminds me that "life will be richer or poorer by the way you use today." That thought might be varied to say: life will be richer or poorer depending on the people you meet today. Most days—and this was one—the people who touch our lives make it richer indeed.

Such a person was the very petite woman who sat in her rocker, poised and unruffled by the many well-wishers who flocked around her. She, for one, took quite in stride the fact that this day she had completed exactly one hundred years of life. Despite the increased longevity our civilization has achieved, a full century of life is still pretty mind-boggling to most of us. Whatever your age, you can speculate in awe the prospect of life stretching on another quarter or half a century, or even three-quarters or more.

It is particularly wonderful when the one-hundred-year-old is still as well, alert and charming as Kate Kasbar. I don't understand people who shudder at the thought of living so long. Given reasonable health and a keen mind, I would hope to pursue in the final quarter century the study of all sorts of things I haven't yet found time for. Some years ago at a DAR luncheon, one of my daughters and I met such a woman who, in her very late years, had learned Greek, continued her study of the piano and several other such scholarly endeavors.

When I bade Kate Kasbar farewell and "happy birthday" today, I took her hand and said I would return next year to photograph her on her next birthday. She smiled, grasped my hand more firmly, and declared, "That's a bargain!" And my life was richer today for having met such a delightful person.

Lynne, an early assistant at the *Independent*.

The young woman whom I bade a fond farewell today was very much a part of my life for most of the past year. Actually, she had been during her entire life, as the daughter of a good friend and a good friend of a daughter.

But nearly a year ago a new relationship developed when she joined me in the writing and production of the *Independent*. It was good from the start and remained so. When I asked her if she would care to join me in this endeavor, it was because I thought she possessed the three qualities most needed: she was intelligent, articulate and enthusiastic. The first two would be as nothing without the third.

Lynne Shakshober's progress with the paper is certainly too well-known to all who read her writing, gave her advertising assignments or merely met her in her daily rounds (every single day of the week and most nights) to require description here. Her enthusiasm and friendliness endeared her to them; her enthusiasm and ever cheerful disposition endeared her to those who worked with her.

It will be lonely in this solitary editorial tower this week. Working and planning together and discussing the next move—or the last one—created a companionship that will be missed and always remembered fondly.

When I look across the desk now, she is not there, and I miss her. But she has gone on her way, as young people must. She left a bit of her heart with the *Independent*, and just as when our very own young people left home, a bit of our heart went with her. But she, too, made my days richer.

Good luck, little grasshopper!

A Man This Town Needed

July 2, 1981

A few years ago, a series of editorials ran on this page under the heading "What This Town Needs." The pieces didn't provoke the amount of reaction one might have hoped, but in the files was one letter in response, which went like this:

"The town needs me…because I like the town and the townspeople and I think they like me…and because I have something to offer that many townspeople would like; compassion, concern, respect, old time novelty music, the Gospel and Friendship…because the townspeople offer me and my family a beautiful kind of life."

The letter concluded with this explanation: "What this town needs is me… nobody will disclaim this if he puts himself in the category of 'me.' We need each other to make the town continue to be as good or better than it is."

This practical interpretation of what this town needs came from a man who indeed gave in full measure all those things which he claimed to give. Giving them the Gospel was, of course, Reverend Gayle Miller's life's work, but it was the compassion, concern, respect and friendship freely dispensed along with it that gave the Gospel its proper meaning. And none of this was reserved only for members of his congregations. He was a gregarious man, and he shared himself unselfishly with everyone in the community, regardless of religious persuasion. He spent a lot of time in the hospitals visiting the sick, and he visited everyone from the Roe Jan area, not only his own church people. Nor did he confine his visiting to the hospitals. If anyone was ill at home or simply sad or lonely, he had time to visit them, too, to offer a prayer and a cheerful word.

Next to the Gospel and people, one of the things that seemed to give Reverend Miller great pleasure was that old-time music he speaks of. I shall always remember him presiding over an old-fashioned hymn sing in his church. I shall have to dig out the picture that appeared in the *Independent* some day to recall just how many instruments he really was playing. He was surely playing a guitar and harmonica, and I think a saxophone—I don't remember what else, but oh, wasn't he having fun? And in his kindly way, he brought happiness to those in Pine Haven Home with his musical visits there.

But while it may have seemed that this man was all upfront, that everything about him could be seen on the surface, there was another person hidden inside the happy and joking exterior—a craftsman and a poet. Many people in this area are familiar with the woodcarving he enjoyed as a hobby, and some have certainly read his poems, for his written work occasionally appeared on this page. One we happened to run across this week might well be his epitaph, for it so well expresses his philosophy in a simple way. Speaking of the Lord, who, he says, "went around doing good," Reverend Miller laments that "it is frustrating for us to find that we, trying to be like him, are just going around!" But then he admonishes us to also do good "and complete the circle of friendship and joy in the time of eternity!"

His circle here on earth has been completed, but it's our guess that Gayle Miller is now making lots of friends in eternity.

A "New" Kind of Medicine?

June 4, 2009

If you were watching the USA Network on TV recently, you saw a probably engaging young actor playing the role of a physician in a "new original series" about "concierge" medicine. His character and role were touted in the advance publicity as a doctor who "cares deeply and passionately about his chosen profession." He has time for his patients and actually knows them, their background and family. In addition to other good things, the publicity says the patients get more "face time."

So this is new? Let us introduce you to one of our local doctors who never heard that "concierge" referred to physicians. (They may remember that

The man known to all as "Doc." *Courtesy of Helen Hall.*

person is in charge at a French hotel.) In those days (before managed care), this concierge-style medicine was known as general practice and people had a "family doctor."

When someone in the family didn't feel well, the doctor's office was called. You probably didn't get an appointment to see the doctor; you simply appeared in his waiting room for his office hours and waited your turn. Or if you kept a sick child home from school, you called the office. But you didn't take the child to sit in a crowded waiting room next to other sniffly kids who were sneezing their germs around. No, your young one was kept warm and comfortable in bed, and your doctor came to see him.

Surely there were doctors like this all around the country, but in the Roe Jan area, and beyond, it was Dr. Bowerhan, fondly known to his patients as

"Doc." When he came on a cold winter day to visit a youngster in bed, he opened his black bag, took out his stethoscope and cupped it in his hands to warm it before placing it on a feverish chest. He knew these children, most likely having been there when they were born since obstetrics was his specialty. And he very likely hung around the hospital for a while before the little one chose to make its entrance into the world. (Of course, there was the one who greeted the world in Doc's car when he decided an expectant mother needed a ride.)

Doc knew his patients, which the concierge doctors are apparently learning as an aid in diagnosis. He not only knew them and their medical histories well, but he very likely knew their whole families, what illnesses they had and even their temperaments, excitable about illnesses or not.

Doc loved practicing medicine, and he practiced it twenty-four hours a day. He was always available to his patients. Sometimes he'd turn up at a social gathering where his wife had preceded him, but he was restless. He personified that old expression, like "a hen on a hot griddle," until the phone rang. The operators (who are another story) had tracked him down, and he seemed relieved to be back in his car on his way to care for a patient.

He did have a couple of hobbies that fit his lifestyle. Doc loved his cars, he spent so much time in them, and the vehicles got sportier as the years went by. He also enjoyed photography, often taking photos on his rounds and developing the film in his darkroom.

Doc also made hospital visits. The new trend in hospitals is to have a physician, called a hospitalist, permanently on staff since a patient's own doctor isn't always there. But Doc was there every day around noon, saw his patient, grabbed lunch with another physician who was his friend and dashed back home to hold office hours, sometimes looking in on a sick child along the way.

Patients of concierge doctors pay an annual fee. Doc was pretty informal about bills and sometimes was paid with a dozen eggs from the farm, for example, if the patient had more eggs than cash.

There was a time when just about every baby born in this area was a Dr. Bowerhan baby. Sometime after he had died (while working) these babies contributed in his name to a birthing room at the hospital where they were born.

Since Doc didn't take time off to travel, he may never have heard of a concierge, but he could tell these new doctors a few things about "face time."

Remembering a Friend

April 26, 1984

I remember the first time I met Ernie. It was at a meeting on the proposed zoning law for Hillsdale. Those gatherings tended toward mild hysteria, but that evening there was one particularly calm and sensible voice in the crowd. As a reporter, I sought out the speaker as the crowd dispersed in order to put a name with a quote. It was Ernie Seligmann.

I next came across him at another meeting at the Craryville Firehouse. I think it had something to do with candidates or maybe sludge or the school—no matter; Ernie was interested in everything in his country community. We talked afterward in the parking lot, and he expressed his interest in the *Independent*. In fact, he had already written earlier to welcome it to the local scene and express his understanding of the great amount of work and long hours behind each issue.

Ernie spent summers reporting for the paper.

Sometime after that, he asked about spending some time working for the paper while at his home here. I stopped by on Tory Hill Road one day, and we talked, not only of that possibility but also of many other things. We spoke, from the start, of things both serious and sublime, and we laughed a lot, too, at the ridiculous.

Ernie came to us many a summer, putt-putting along on a motor scooter much of the time. He came first when we were in the cramped quarters of our first office, and he rejoiced another summer in our move to spacious new quarters where we could enjoy a summer lunch break under the trees. His very first assignment was to cover a tragic accident that took several lives and shook the community. He shot rolls of film, marveled at the work of rescue people and got the story, but said, in describing the scene and those who witnessed it, that "all we could do was weep."

The fine teacher, whose special love was journalism, covered for the *Independent* everything from concerts, places to visit, school and town meetings, to the Democratic convention in New York and life at the Laundromat, commenting meanwhile on the pleasures and puzzlement of life in his column Up Tory Hill. He was serious about it all, but it was fun, too—oh, such fun it was.

Best of all, for all of us, was Ernie's unswerving friendship. I once apologized for inconveniencing him on a day when he didn't usually work with us and his reply was, "It's all right—I'm your friend." And what is more precious than a true friend?

Ernie claimed he couldn't go to bed at night without reading the *New York Times*, and his family honored that respect when they placed the notice of his death in its pages last week. But while he loved to read the *Times*, he loved the *Independent* in a different way, for he was part of it; thus it was here that the story of his life and death was told.

Last June, Ernie returned to celebrate the tenth anniversary of this newspaper with us, and again later in the summer to reminisce about those ten years. He won't be coming any more, claimed quite suddenly by cancer—that cruel disease that had already cut short the young life of another member of our staff. But we shall continue to speak and think of him often as we continue weekly that work he loved. He was a good man.

CHAPTER 4

Seasons

Spring Things

April 29, 1976

Spring is perhaps the most welcome of seasons, and it consists of a number of things:

Birdsong to awaken by on sunny mornings; treetops filled with birds; the churring of redwings, the chirping of robins, a cardinal whistling.

Tiny yellow coltsfoot blooming in the gravel at the road's edge; dogtooth violets at the roadside; purple and white violets running rampant through the garden.

Crab apple blossoms and bright flowering quince in dooryards; bright red tulips circling a tree on a neat front lawn.

A clump of columbine leaves; the first blood-red trillium and pure white bloodroot.

A south wind warning of rain, carrying the voices of the cattle across the fields.

The mountain hidden by a misty blowing cloud.

A grey squirrel darting up a tree, pausing and disappearing into an unseen crack.

Kids on bikes; a little boy riding "no-hands" with his shirt tied around his waist; the sun tanning his bare back.

Lawn mowers tuning up for the busy season ahead; and lilac buds getting ready for a fragrant May.

A little girl amid wild flowers.

Covers coming off backyard pools; and ice-nudged docks being straightened up along the lakeshore.

Daffodils and elderberry bushes flowering; the delicate shadblow embroidering the forest with its lacy blooms.

A color card of greens and reds trimming the branches of budding trees; the graceful dogwood, with its branches lying gently like arms outstretched and the palm upward.

Snowy mountains overlooking the green valley.

Skunk cabbage in the low woodlands; onion grass in the lawn.

Rabbits in the garden; ants in the kitchen.

New ferns uncurling beside last summer's perfectly dried stalks.

Mountain pink making a splash of color on the banks along driveways; wash billowing on clotheslines.

Sheep on the Langdon farm in Copake.

The perky heads of dandelions dotting the lawn; April showers; and snow showers.

The smell of new mown grass and the earth turned over in the garden; an old apple tree in bud, the first flowering branch in a stoneware bottle on the windowsill.

The bitter and the sweet; the sweetness of a sunny morning as balmy as a Caribbean day; the bitterness of one as chillingly grey as a November day that bodes of winter.

A meadowlark in the field; a scent of flowers in the air; walking again in bare feet and dipping them in the still cold pond.

Robert Browning said it well:

The year's at the spring
And Day's at the morn;
Morning's at seven:
The hillside's dew-pearled;
The lark's on the wing;
The snail's on the thorn:
God's in his heaven—
All's right with the world!

HOME BUILDING TIME IS HERE

May 9, 1974

Our local banks have been advertising homeowners' clubs and loans for home improvements during the past few weeks since this time of year is traditionally spring cleaning, renovation or building time. This is true not only among people but also in the world of nature all around us. There is a great hustle and bustle going on in the bird world outside the door these days. You hear them in the morning, chattering and chirping at a great rate about their doings.

The robins, of course, have already settled in for the first nesting. One has taken up residence in the evergreen tree right outside our front door,

A spider's new home.

as usual. The birds seem to rebuild and improve on what remained of last year's nest, thus losing no time moving in. There are disadvantages, of course, in having a bird nest at your very door. There's always the frightened flight every time the door opens or someone approaches. But if there's a window nearby, it's a good way to be able to watch them and see when the new family first makes its appearance, with their hungry beaks wide open, searching constantly for food—the amount of which the babies consume being nothing short of remarkable.

Last week, dandelions covered the lawn and now are going to seed, so this morning the beautiful little goldfinches that wait for this fluffy down are ready to build their nests. A couple of pairs are busy on the back lawn, tawny golden females and vivid yellow males. There also seems to be something the birds like on the climbing roses.

For the past two or three years, a pair of perky wrens has nested in a gate post near the house, and we're always glad to see them return. One of their first nests still remains at the top of the post just inside its boxing. But each year it seems to like a new location in the same building, which appears to be turning into a high-rise apartment. It's rather comical to watch a little bird doing its spring cleaning, but that's just what our wrens were doing the other day, darting in and out, bringing out bits of last year's bedding to discard. These busy and vociferous little birds are always fun to watch. An amazing amount of sound pours forth from their small throats as they perch on the fence and deliver lengthy speeches.

A handsome male cardinal was on the ground right outside the door this morning, still seeking out the remains of sunflower seeds fallen from the feeder that has been put away for the season. The nest a pair of cardinals made in a bush, just inches from one of our windows, last year withstood most of the winter wind, rain and snow; it only recently has broken up. A few shreds remain, however, and we wonder whether the birds will get the home-building urge to return to it. We certainly hope they will, as we were honored to have them so close last summer.

Surprisingly, the cardinal appeared a few minutes later at a year-round feeder, standing even closer to a window that it usually never goes near, and made off with a sizable piece of dried bread. This may be a good sign that it plans to live near us for the summer months. The chickadees still return hopefully to inspect the tree where the feeder had hung, but they apparently nest far off in the privacy of the woods.

It is always a treat for a birdwatcher to see a new species, one that had never before been viewed in the home area. Last week, there was a different-looking woodpecker working busily at a maple tree, and a quick search through Roger Tory Peterson's *Field Guide* revealed that it was a yellow-bellied sapsucker. We are now on the lookout for the greatest woodpecker of them all, that huge, seventeen- to nineteen-inch crested bird of the woodlands, the pileated woodpecker. Peterson says, "The diggings, large oval or oblong holes, are certain evidence of its presence." We've discovered just such a hole, about a foot high, five inches wide and six inches deep, in a dead tree at the edge of the woods. The enormous hole appears to be freshly made, and on the ground below it is a big pile of wood chips, each about an inch long, that we could spread on the garden instead of buying a bag full of them at the nursery. We shall have to be on constant watch, too, for this seldom-seen wood chopper.

The trees have really come into leaf during the past week. But while this is happening, it is interesting to note the variation in color and texture on a wooded hillside. As trees bud and burst into bloom they are usually very similar in color to their autumn hue. Some of the maple leaves unfurling this past week, for example, were a definite mixture of red and yellow, as they will be in October. Soon our Berkshire foothills will be a solid mass of green; but at this lovely moment, they present a fascinating spectrum of pale and yellowy greens, tinged here and there with red and highlighted by the lacy white branches of the shadblows.

Reminders of last fall remain in marshy spots along the road where once stalwart brown cattails stood. Now they sport pale beige fluffy heads before they disappear to make way for new green plants in the marsh. Those field grasses that appear so red in the early fall have also been rosy, particularly when wet with spring rain.

My beloved dogwood, whose blooms finally appeared after so many barren years, is now blossoming for the third year. I'm afraid some birds that passed by during migration yanked off quite a few of its buds, so it's not exactly spectacular. But after waiting for it to flower for so long, it looks good to me.

Summertime—a Treasure

August 7, 1975

It's midsummer—well, not quite by the calendar—but in the minds of most people, summer is essentially July and August. Therefore, once August 1 has come, it seems like the beginning of the end.

A summer wedding, and the beginning of our life here.

Summer always seems to be the shortest of the four seasons. It appears to arrive at the last minute before July 4 and end abruptly, soon after Labor Day. In fact, we always remember a Labor Day when the children were young and another family came to picnic with us at the lake, which was tradition for Labor Day. It was really cold, and the little ones were all looking quite bundled up in their hooded sweatshirts with the kangaroo pockets (which, now that they're quite grown up, they're wearing again as a new style).

Aside from the fact that we had a dry spell, which is surely not unusual for our summers, followed by a deluge, this has been a pretty nice summer. Some days the past week have been the kind of summer day you dream about in March. The sky has been a cloudless blue; the sun has been bright; and the air has been clear and breezy. The sky has been filled with stars, and one night we saw for an instant what must have been a satellite traveling swiftly across the heavens, quickly disappearing among all the other shining lights up there.

Walking or biking up the lane some evenings, it was absolutely quiet and still. Millions of fireflies twinkled, and the cattle moved soundlessly across the field, with the stillness broken only by the distant sound of a car down on Route 22.

There's something about sitting on the porch on a summer evening, in an old-fashioned rocking chair, of course, which is a sheer delight. The crickets and katydids pursue their chatty conversation relentlessly, and every once in awhile an owl hoots. It's a bit too warm for comfort in the house, but it's perfect on the porch.

In retrospect, it seems that this is the way it was, way back many years ago. There were lots of hot summer days and delightfully warm summer nights. As children then, we put on a clean dress for dinner after a day of swimming at the ore bed and walked to the movies in the evening. We went to the park lots of evenings for a picnic—the woodsy part that isn't even open anymore—especially when there was company visiting. As teenagers, we drank lemon or chocolate cokes ("Small cokes") at Bash Bish Lodge and put nickels in the jukebox to listen and dance to Glenn Miller playing "String of Pearls" and "I Know Why" (not "the Glenn Miller sound," just plain, real Glenn Miller). If the boy with the little Ford runabout came along (who seemed to drive so excitingly fast that it made our mothers nervous), we all piled in—the rumble seat was best—and went joy riding up the road past the falls and back, probably at the incredible speed of thirty-five miles per hour or so.

When the children were young and we spent quite a bit of summer time at the lake, we used to sit on the porch at night, listening to the deep-voiced chorus of frogs. But it seems it was never warm. We were always bundled up—too much like cold summer nights in the Adirondacks. Now perhaps those old-fashioned warm and sunny summers have returned, and aren't they welcome? Not only does it bring back memories, but also it is a joy to savor each lovely sunny day and balmy evening when we can rock on the porch until the late hours or lie back in a patio chair and watch the rosy sunset become a starry night.

Summer here is a treasure, briefly held, before it is gone as suddenly as it came. Enjoy it!

MIDSUMMER RAMBLINGS

July 29, 1976

Why is summer such a fleeting thing? It never seems to arrive any earlier in June than the calendar indicates nor to remain until late September. "In Camelot," so the song goes, "by order summer lingers through September." Not so here.

Horses enjoy the spring sunshine.

Oh, of course it was as hot as a July day should be this past Easter week, and we'll no doubt have the usual Indian summer briefly in October. But between the real summer and those special days are many cool ones.

In fact, we had a touch of September last weekend with record-low temperatures Sunday night. This sort of thing is rather typical of our August, but it was really strange weather for July.

What is it about summer that is so inviting, and why does it seem so ethereal? It must be because we look forward to the balminess of really nice summer weather to act as a balm for our winter-weary selves. Most people take their vacation in summer, looking at the months of more severe weather as the time to work and the hot summer days as the best time to slow down and rest. It is frustrating then, when we don't always get the chance to spend long days relaxing in the summer sunshine after waiting all year for its return. The summer always slips by before there's enough time to partake of its many joys.

First of all, there's warm sunshine, interspersed with soft breezes and the cool shade of big old trees. There's cool, clear water to swim in or drift on in a boat. There are mild nights when one can sit out under the stars, and there have been beautiful starry nights this past week. There are fresh fruits and vegetables in good supply, and best of all, there's the sweet corn that's worth waiting a whole year for. Kids can get ice cream more often, and the tinkling bell of the ice cream truck is a very special summer sound.

Sitting on the porch is a special treat of summer. Every house should have a porch or verandah, especially in the country, with real, old-fashioned rockers and maybe a hammock or porch swing. It's the most relaxing place for reading, visiting with neighbors or just "settin' and rockin'," a summer pastime everyone could use more of to calm their work-weary nerves. No modern invention for relaxing tired muscles, nor any tranquilizing pill, can beat the old porch rocker for making a body forget its aches, pains and problems.

But, as mentioned on this page a few weeks ago, when summer seemed only to have started, there is so much to do in the summer and so many places to go. This is a great place for vacationers to fill their leisure hours after getting their fill of swimming, boating, fishing, hiking and picnicking. For then they can go to the church fairs, flea markets, carnivals, movies, concerts, plays, etc.—all the things we do when we go away on vacation but never seem to find enough time to do here at home. When shall we ever arrange to take a vacation in our own Berkshires like so many other thousands from other places do?

There are deer grazing in the fields every evening, looking so red against the green of the alfalfa or the stubble of newly mown hay. They look up curiously and go back to eating, finally deciding maybe we're not good company and then bounding away.

From the nearby hilltop, one can watch the summer lights come on below, the red letters on the movie marquee and the headlights of country-bound, Friday-night traffic. The sound of music can be heard from over in the camping area of the park. The songbirds murmur a good night song as the stars begin to appear. It's a lovely season to be living in the country. If only we could make it stand still for awhile so that we could savor it longer.

THE LAST WORD ON AUGUST

September 2, 1982

For the past several weeks, editors everywhere have been waxing poetic about the month of August, and a lot of prose has been written about its warm and lazy days, from the Sunday *Times* to neighboring weeklies.

In old days, farmers shared a thresher that worked at each farm.

Some have mentioned that it's changeable, covering all bases, in fact, by suggesting that it might be sunny or rainy, it might be cool but then again warm, etc. Several years ago, this column was written about the "Brr-erkshire" weather at this time of year, specifically August, and it could as well have been published again during the past few weeks, especially now after last weekend's record low.

I have spent summers here my entire life, and it's always the same. If we didn't have a calendar, we'd still know when it was August. The days change—the air is clearer and cooler. Sure, it was rainy during mid-August this year, but mostly August is bright-blue sky, warm sun and cool air. Just sit around in a wet bathing suit as the sun goes lower in the sky or disappears behind a few slow-moving clouds, and you'll see how warm August is here. No more is the grass warm under bare feet nor is the porch floor pleasantly cool underfoot: it's downright chilly.

And the nights; we know it's August when we can no longer sit on the porch for dinner without a warm sweater, and everyone who comes for the weekend starts pulling out quilts at bedtime (or when they wake up shivering in the early morning hours). These are the cold August nights, followed by brisk mornings. The days warm up beautifully, but mornings are pretty cool.

Then there are the sounds that tell us it's August, even when we forget to turn the calendar page. Even before the sunsets the humming begins, not the "peepers" of early spring but the steady singers of August. And as dusk overtakes us on our walk to watch the deer grazing calmly on the alfalfa in the fields, the sound increases in volume as the tenors and basses among these little tree creatures join the sopranos of early evening. Some hum continuously, others seem to converse back and forth in rasping tones. They are nature's "New Swingle Singers," playing their August booking in the country.

There are the fragrances of August: the pungent smell of the ripening corn and the sweet smell of second- and third-cutting hay just mowed and still laying in the field. There are colors of August, too: the beautiful sky blue of the chicory growing along the roadsides, as if reflecting the sky itself; the orange tinge of the sunlight touching those leaves already beginning to turn to autumn colors; the tawny goldenrod; and the lovely mauve of Joe Pye Weed in the wet places.

This is August in our countryside.

September Song

September 30, 1980

September—it's a melancholy month and an unsettled time. The days begin to change, losing the feel of summer as soon as Labor Day has gone by. Some days are cold, warning of fall coming soon. The lingering summer we hoped for ends abruptly.

Often it is a month of hurricanes, but just as it happened here early this week—a night of wind and rain, littering the lawn with fallen leaves and branches, and felling row upon row of tall corn—can be followed suddenly by a warm and summery day. Suddenly it is seventy degrees and sticky, just when the pool has been let down and covered for winter, after two weeks that were too cold for swimming. Such are the disappointments of September.

The house grows cold and damp, and we suffer a bit of a chill; we are loath to turn on the heat and admit that the season has changed. The clothes in the closet are all wrong—something that was bright and cheerful a few weeks ago now makes you look like the last rose of summer. In younger days, we welcomed the change into bright fall woolens. Now we hang back, trying not to rush the season.

Above: Harvest time with the farmer's favorite team.

Right: Hired man Joe pushes feed to his clean cows.

The light is different in September. Sandwiched between the crisp, golden, blue-skied days of August and October, it is hazy and the light is diffused by that haze. A mist hides the mountain in the morning, slowly rising, as dew glistens on the grass. The days grow short, as the song says. Twilight comes earlier, with tree toads playing their final rasping refrain.

There is something wistful about September, a longing perhaps for summer to stay longer while we hear of a severe winter coming. Sad things seem to happen in September, and some days we wonder why we're melancholy. The Day of Atonement sometimes comes in September.

Elsewhere in this issue, Walt Whitman is quoted on the season and aptly describes "the September breeze, with pensive cadence through the treetops." Yet there is a stillness about September that makes it seem that we are suspended in time and space, a waiting time between seasons. Pensive—that describes the September mood so well; it is a time to reflect on summer days and to look ahead to the quickening of the season ahead.

CHAPTER 5
Newspaper

Big Moments for RJI

March 13, 1980

It was just four years ago, in March 1976, when, as perhaps the newest and youngest member of the New York Press Association, the Roe Jan *Independent* won its first award. I should say awards because, with beginner's luck, the *Independent* won two the first time it was entered in the association's annual Better Newspaper Contest.

Entering the contest is a big job. First, the list of classes (now totaling twenty-three) must be carefully studied. Then, all fifty-one issues of the contest year (October 1–September 30) must be studied very thoroughly to determine which classes should be entered and, by a long process of elimination, which articles, issues or photos to enter. It has been suggested that every newspaper office should have a box in which any issue containing a possible entry should be set aside as it's published, thus making the search for entries much easier when they are due. This, of course, is one of those good intentions we never seem to get around to fulfilling.

So when the time comes, we're too busy with pre-Christmas issues, too busy grabbing every possible moment of relaxation during our one week off after Christmas and too busy getting back into the swing of things after our holiday to begin to prepare to enter the contest. Thus, it is usually on the very last day that our entry is packed up and postmarked.

I shall always remember that first year for special and sentimental reasons. The deadline was a month or two earlier than it is now. Service to

The Roe Jan *Independent* displays awards in its office window.

The editor with then governor Malcolm Wilson, *center*, and Copake supervisor Ellsworth Weaver, *left*.

Agriculture was a new and open class, not separated into divisions according to circulation. I made some other entries, too, but this was the main class in which I thought—or hoped—this fledgling newspaper stood a chance of perhaps an honorable mention.

When I had finally assembled my entries, they needed to be sent in a box since the Agricultural entry required a scrapbook of clippings, and it was a pretty big one. My father wasn't well then, but he was good at that sort of thing, and he packed it all up for me to mail. How I wished he were still living on that exciting day a few months later when this paper, in which he took such pride, was presented two first-place awards!

That year the annual convention was held on Long Island, and the awards were presented at a luncheon. The officer making the presentations always begins at the end of the list, announcing winners beginning with honorable mention in each class, then third, etc.

By the time I'd heard those two called, my heart sank. We hadn't even managed to place. A paper out of Suffolk County took second, and then first—Roe Jan *Independent*! To say it was an exciting moment is an understatement, for sure. But it was pretty well matched when this newspaper was called again for first place in its division for Best Front Page.

This year, preparing the entries was made easier by the good assistance of a determined assistant editor whose help made it possible to enter more classes. They were even mailed a day or two ahead of the deadline. Those of us who went to the awards banquet were all delighted when we were called for first place in Service to Agriculture and again when we made first in Best Special Section for our division. Working toward the top of the prize list, the announcer finally reached the first category and place actually listed: in Division One for General Excellence, Roe Jan *Independent*. We were ecstatic!

This was the first time the *Independent* had been entered in that class because the editor had always run out of steam before getting that far. Thanks to Diane, we entered, and thanks to the entire staff and its contributors, we made it to the top.

Now we finally have the box, and if we can just find time to set aside possible entries, we'll be on our way to trying for a win next year.

Newspapers Are Good For...

September 19, 1985

Occasionally, the *Independent* runs a tongue-in-cheek list of things newspapers are good for, like wrapping fish and covering the floor while you paint. But seriously, there should be a lot of good reading before the newspaper reaches those final uses. Newspapers are the greatest sources of information; they are far more complete and detailed than other instant news sources such as TV and radio.

But while a big-city newspaper provides a lot more floor coverage for the paint job and can mulch a huge vegetable garden (shredded or otherwise), it is the community newspaper that fills a particular need for information that no other media really touch. A particularly bad accident or other disaster may get a quick spot on the "local" TV channels (tucked in among all the

Dick served as ad salesman and office manager.

lurid details of Capital District crime) and once in awhile the *New York Times* (or *Newsday*!) drops in to do a feature on some quaint aspect of rural life.

Meanwhile, it is the country weekly, the hometown community newspaper that provides information about life in that community—the actions of its town officials and school boards, the activities of its churches and schools, important events in the lives of its people, notices of all kinds of interesting things to do and places to visit in the local area, helpful information for farmers and gardeners, reports on Little Leaguers and tournament golfers, features on local people and places, special supplements featuring agriculture (our most important industry) and country living, publicity on the fundraisers of community organizations, photos and firsthand reports on festivals, frolics, floods, fires and election fights.

It is rather appropriate that National Newspaper Week falls this year at a time when this community newspaper has the final wrap-up of political caucuses in the local towns. This is the people's opportunity to be involved in government at the grass roots—where it all begins—as voters and candidates for office. It is encouraging to see that in most cases the two-, or even three-party system is being kept alive, providing the voter with contests, even if not as thriving as it might be if full slates were fielded in all cases. But be assured that the community newspaper will be one of the best sources of information about those candidates so that voters may be informed before going to the polls, hopefully to cast their ballot for that candidate they consider best for the job, regardless of party affiliation.

Despite TV, radio and newspaper chains, the locally owned community newspapers keep on growing, even in the neighborhoods of cities. The Roe Jan *Independent*, now in its thirteenth year, continues to provide a window on the world and an intimate look at the world of the Roe Jan community.

Of Wednesdays and Women

June 11, 1981

It was a Wednesday night, eight years ago, a warm one, as I recall. Paper sheets we call flats were laid out on my dining room table and, armed with cans of rubber cement, we were pasting up the first issue of the new weekly newspaper, the Roe Jan *Independent*. Rubber cement, incidentally, is not good for the finish on a dining room table. The light spots it made cleared up after awhile, but the memory of the adventure of those early days lingers on.

Daughter Meg and Ernie work on layout.

An often appearing filler, many readers recognized the editor' s family name.

That was only the beginning of a long succession of Wednesdays, and I never got home for dinner on that night of the week for the first five years or more. More midnight oil than rubber cement and printers' ink seemed to be required to turn out a newspaper every week. But the paper has grown, widened its coverage, won quite a few prizes and has become a household word in a community where there's a reason to look forward to every Thursday.

For pretty obvious reasons, this anniversary issue has always featured women, and we never seem to run out of interesting women in this community. We have featured women at home and at work, as volunteers, in the church, as horsewomen, as mothers and as farmers. The list goes on and on. As some of the women interviewed for today's issue point out, it's rather amazing what women have accomplished, considering the odds against them. But more and more, women are realizing that they can do just about anything they want to do if they try hard enough, and gradually, with a new generation, the odds are swinging a little more in their favor. (I speak with some authority, mind you, having five daughters doing great things.)

Perhaps the greatest male chauvinist of them all, the legendary Henry Higgins of *My Fair Lady*, wondering in song, "Why Can't A Woman Be Like A Man?" boasts of men that they are such "a marvelous sex." Well, we like them, too, but what a dull world they would have without not only the company but also the challenge of the ladies, God bless them!

Country Editor's Weekend

December 9, 1976

It's Friday afternoon, and in offices everywhere, people are saying "so long; see you Monday—have a nice weekend." It has snowed, and it looks like a fine weekend ahead for winter sports, Christmas shopping or just curling up by the fire with a good book.

But up in the newspaper office, the light still burns as the working day winds slowly down, and the camera is loaded to take some late-afternoon photos. Outside, the hills turn a rose color in the reflected glow of a lovely sunset, creating in a country editor an intense longing to be out there and enjoying the beauty of the day's end.

Finally there comes a moment of decision to head for home, possibly catching the last few moments of afterglow on the new snow in a quick tour

Cross-country skiing, which is an after-work relaxation.

of the nearby fields on skis. However, by the time a hasty search has been made for the boots put carefully away last spring, the sun is gone and darkness comes quickly. But all is not lost, for a beautiful full moon has come up, with a bright star shining beside it in the clear sky. In the beauty of the evening, there is a sudden release from cares while striding across the moonlit field and a solace of solitude when standing to look up at the mountain; the sky is a balm to the weary spirit. It's time to head home now to prepare dinner.

Saturday: It is a snowy and busy day, with more pictures to take, a few office chores to do and a trip to Hudson to do the legwork for a report on one of our advertisers. A few errands can be sandwiched in along the way, but finally it's back home again to grab a quick sandwich, make an ad call and maybe get a little writing done. Another brief jaunt on the skis at nightfall, with the destination being the nearby church, finally brings a leisure moment at day's end.

Sunday dawns; it is bright and clear. After a few household chores are complete, it's off to take pictures again of Roe Jan people and places, which fills the rest of the day. An ad is arranged during a friendly fireside visit, and news is picked up here and there along the way on this delightful sunny December day. Little kids are out with sleds, and big and small alike are enjoying the newly covered ski slopes.

In the late afternoon, it's time to head for the final picture-taking assignment for the day. The sun is setting again, and two jets streak the wintry sky above the pale pink glow wreathing the hills. Lights are beginning to come on in the barns as farmers prepare for the evening milking. As the sun disappears, it grows cold, and the people gathering for the lighting of a Christmas tree draw close to the wood fires to warm themselves. Candles are lighted, and carols are sung, with the faces of little children shining expectantly in the light of candles that are clutched in their mittened hands.

And then, at the prescribed moment, the lights go on for the first time of this blessed season. Friends and kinfolk visit briefly together before heading home for their dinner and the comfort of their firesides. The moon again shines brightly ("on the breast of the new fallen snow"), and when it's time to turn out the lights this night, there is certainly the "luster of midday" on the whole countryside.

It's time to turn in and get ready to get back to work tomorrow. It's been a busy weekend, and one that left no time to be busy at home with very necessary things like cleaning the house before Christmas decorating or baking cookies. But it was not such a bad weekend really—just pretty typical for a country editor.

Hope you had a good weekend, too.

Rambling On

September 8, 1983

The Sixth Annual Roe Jan Ramble has come and gone, and some of the workers are nearly as tired as the runners were when they crossed the finish line. Handling the entries for over two hundred people takes a lot of time and a high degree of organization. Marking the course and erecting signs is another chore, and timing the runners and guiding them so that scorekeepers

The editor, *right*, with a runner at one of the annual Roe Jan Rambles.

can be absolutely accurate takes skill and energy. Finally, tabulation of runners' names and times takes absolute concentration. Many volunteers are involved in all of this, from mailing out entry blanks, to making posters, to carting tables to the entry points and to collecting pins and numbers to be used again another year.

And then there are the women who furnish the runners with a cool drink at the end of the race, and the Cub Scouts who stand patiently along the course, with their arms outstretched, holding cups of water for the runners to refresh themselves as they hurry by and even giving an occasional shower or hose set up by kind and interested residents along their route to give them a moment's relief from the heat of the road.

Firefighters and police control the traffic to make the way safe for the runners, from little tots of preschool age to their grandfathers—all running together; the Rescue Squad follows along, just in case of an injury that puts someone out of the running.

Runners enjoyed the 6.2-mile run through farm country.

When it's all over for all of the above, the work continues for the staff of the *Independent*, which sponsors the Ramble and gives it extensive coverage. The many photos of runners and volunteers must be developed; contacts are printed for thorough study; decisions and choices are made; everything is returned for printing (all of which means several trips to and from Great Barrington); and then we figure out how to fit them all in this issue!

The Ramble went well this year, as it always does. Runners praise the course and the dedication of the volunteers who make everything run smoothly for them. Some expressed regret that they no longer had the excitement of running down the main street of Copake to be greeted by a cheering crowd near the finish line. The crowd at the town hall was smaller, of course, without the addition of shoppers who came to town and decided to watch the race while buying their groceries, ice, gas or the morning paper when it ended at the *Independent*'s office. But their friends and lots of neighbors from that area lined the route along the finish line to cheer them on, and they appreciated the shade of the big old oak that greeted them there, which was a grassy place to sit and watch their fellow runners come in.

Both runners and volunteers, and the sponsor of the Ramble, appreciate the cooperation of the Copake Town Board in welcoming the Ramble to uptown Copake and even having one board member run!

"THE STRING IS ON THE BOX"

June 9, 1983

At the moment this is written, the 10th anniversary issue of the Roe Jan *Independent*, the 51st this volume year, the 510th paper written, photographed, set in type, pasted up and printed since that exciting day ten years ago, is on its way "to bed." And before many more hours go by, all those involved in the production of these thirty-two pages that must be on the newsstands tomorrow at noon will be wishing that they, too, were *literally* on their way to bed. For this anniversary week has been one of many fraught with obstacles, yet there has always been an *Independent* on the newsstands on Thursday for the past ten years. Sometimes staff members have had doubts about that possibility, but the editor merely says, "The paper always comes out." And so it does, although one never knows just when that will be—not until as the editor happened to say recently, "the string is on the box" (in which it goes to the printer).

Readers of this newspaper have heard more than once, on anniversary days, of that first issue whose layout was done on the dining room table. Staff members from the earliest days surely recall the amount of midnight oil required to get the paper out, and the meals and sleep that were missed. With a larger staff, there are more people to share the work of each week, but with a larger paper, there's more work. Early along, a reader commented that it seemed our two reporters had been *everywhere* within a week, and it still seems that way. The paper has been instrumental in bringing about good things in the community, to say nothing of first of all creating an informed public.

People laugh when they hear, "in the beginning we had one desk and took turns sitting at it," but those who watched the beginning of the *Independent* will remember that it was really true. We graduated to two desks, then a whole room and finally, five years ago, much larger quarters, with not only more work space, but more wall space for the plaques that are filling it up.

The *Independent* office in Copake.

Yet, as is stated elsewhere in this issue, none will ever equal the feeling when the first two were announced: "First place, Roe Jan *Independent*." Have you ever seen an editor jump out of her skin?

Many people have done a good job for the *Independent* over the years, for which the editor is grateful, and the countless favors of running film to and fro, taking a picture when staff members couldn't spread themselves far enough, carrying the camera-ready flats to the printer early Thursday morning when a weary staff welcomed sleeping in a little longer; all of these are such wonderful expressions of interest in this hometown newspaper that, believe it or not, this editor is at a loss for words.

Just let it be said that it's been fun, there's been a good deal of pride in doing it, and hopefully the *Independent* will go on forever, always growing bigger and better. For the community support and interest and enthusiasm—thank you. And won't you please stop by at our open house this Friday afternoon so we can say it in person?

CHAPTER 6

FAMILY

THE HEART OF THE HOME

December 5, 1985

One evening recently a friend walked past our kitchen table and, smiling knowingly, commented, "Two placemats." She knew from experience what that signifies: most generally only two at the table, so why bother even putting them away between meals when the setting will be the same next time? And she knew well what a change this is from former times when a large family gathered at the table for every evening meal.

For one thing, a larger table was needed then, and in this household, which does not have a "formal" dining room, it was the long sawbuck table in the dining room—the room in which the family virtually lived. I recall reading at the time the house was planned and built that in colonial homes such a room was called a "keeping room." And the table was the center of that room, really the heart of the home.

For it was there that not only the always important gathering for dinner took place, but also so many other things were done by all members of the family. It was, of course, the place to do homework, when—even though you had a desk in your room—you preferred company. It was the place to lay out patterns and fabric to cut a dress and place at one end (funny, it was always the same end) the sewing machine. It was the place to spread out any kind of work, from the family bookkeeping to writing Christmas cards—and, of course, it was where Christmas gifts were wrapped.

It was—and is—one family member's place for any creative writing to be done; no other place will do. It's the ample space for laying out geodetic maps to plan a hike or measure a ski trail. It's served as a center for club meetings and business conferences. It's a good place for playing games and sorting out pictures to put in a photo album. It's also the place to set up the projector for family slide presentations, and the place where children played.

Moreover, it was on this table that the first issue of the *Independent* was pasted up nearly thirteen years ago. And it was on this table that a year's worth of issues have been gone over for weeks at a time in years past while making choices to enter in the annual New York Press Association contest.

There are lots of memories attached to this table. It was built by our first neighbor, Eddie Houghtaling Sr. when we lived in our first house, to match a bench we received as a wedding gift. It served us in that first little home and came with us as the family grew, and we moved to larger quarters. One corner must still bear some mark where a little one received a terrible bump on the head during a brother–sister chase, and until it was sanded and refinished some years ago you could read in the soft pine what had been written on homework papers with ballpoint pens. Tiny things like the sewing pins collected in the spaces between its three long boards and had to be cleaned out periodically.

Every home must have a table like this—the gathering place, the heart of the home—in the kitchen, dining room or wherever. When we sit at it to eat most evenings, now one of us moves from our traditional place at one end (mothers and fathers *always* get to sit at the end) to cut down on the passing distance. But on many weekends and holidays it is again crowded with as many as ten, and a new generation now hides under it and climbs up on the benches to set out dishes for the dolls. And so life goes on around the family table.

Bread in the Refrigerator

August 23, 1979

The tin-lined drawer rattles as it's pulled open and rattles as it's shut—a sound of emptiness.

"Where's the bread?" calls the voice of a visiting grownup child, with a hint of disbelief in the voice. No bread—in this house, how can there be no bread?!

"It's in the refrigerator," is the answer.

Packed for the fall trip to college.

The bread is in the refrigerator—in this house? Incredible! There's only one reason to put bread in a refrigerator—to keep it fresh and edible when it hangs around for quite awhile without being eaten. And that happens only in a pretty empty house. But there it is on the refrigerator shelf, not the large family-size loaf either, just a small loaf of bread dwindling down slowly as the chill fights off encroaching mold.

Bread in the refrigerator. Who would have thought about it ever happening here?

But happen it does, eventually, in every household, and this is the time of year for it. It's most apt to happen as the summer wanes and the tenor of life seems to slow down to a lull before the quickening pace of fall. The heat of early summer is gone, the many activities of summer draw to a close, and as the golden days of August replace the heat and humidity of July, nature itself seems quiet.

The midsummer hum of crickets and all those other musical creatures forms a pianissimo background to the gentle breeze stirring the leaves, with a red or gold one falling here and there. Except for a passing car, it is quiet; and while the days are lovely in late August, there is yet a certain air of melancholy pervading them—a sense of impending loss.

For some it signals the end of a holiday time and a loss of that lovely fleeting freedom. For others, it is the time of year when life grows quiet as the family is fragmented, those who have visited go back to their own homes, the younger ones go off each day, though they still return, and the ones just reaching maturity go off to make their own way in the world: to college, the service or a job. It may be just the first one leaving home; even so there's a change to which the remaining family must adjust and a certain sense of loss when one member is missing. Or it might be the last one to go or the only child. (How did one child ever consume so many loaves of bread?) But the time comes.

There is bread in the refrigerator. Who would have thought of it ever happening?

Kids—Who Needs Them?

October 21, 1976

Kids.

They start right off in life by keeping you up nights, and they don't stop.

They tie you down and really restrict your freedom.

When they're little, they want lots of attention; when they think they're quite grown up, they pay no attention to you.

If you want to hug them, they want to squirm away.

When you long for peace and quiet, the little ones are making noise and the big ones don't know how to turn down the stereo.

When it's 2:00 a.m. and you're dying for sleep, they're crying for a feeding; when it's 2:00 a.m. and you're worrying about teenagers dying on the highway, you're aching to hear the sound of their voices at the door.

They keep you sitting in hospital waiting rooms: waiting for them to get born, to get stitches, to get tonsils out or to get casts on.

They cost you money constantly: for getting born, for having shots, for toys, for candy, for education, for camp, for cars or for weddings.

At first it seems they'll never begin to talk; later, it often seems they never stop.

Sometimes it's hard to get them to talk to you, and it's even harder to get them to listen.

At certain ages, they are sure that they know everything.

Kids we all need.

They seldom seem to appreciate anything the older generation does for them.

They cause you all kinds of worry and lots of work.

At one age, they won't eat; at another, they never stop.

These are just some of the things about them.

On the other hand:

They are sweet, funny, roguish, unpredictable, interesting, charming, loyal and lovable.

They help in your later years to prevent the freedom of loneliness.

They come home to visit and keep you up half the night talking.

They greet you with great hugs when they return from their adventures with the outside world and later bring home little ones to again wriggle away when you want to hug them.

They sit in hospital waiting rooms with you when you need comfort and companionship.

They send you money from their paycheck to repay a loan you've long since forgotten.

They suddenly show wisdom and good judgment, seeing things with a fresh clear view.

They make Mother's and Father's Day cards in first grade that choke you up, send you the biggest valentine in the store when they're ten, and when they toast you on your twenty-fifth or fiftieth wedding anniversary, you find it hard to speak.

They surprise you with a birthday cake they make when they're eight and a gourmet dinner when they're eighteen.

If you're sick, they pitch in and cook, run the family business, do the chores and bring you breakfast in bed.

They sympathize with you if things are sad; reassure you when you are worried; and make you smile when you don't think you feel like it.

They sometimes make you so proud, you could burst.

Who needs them?

They may seem a bother, an expense and a population threatener at times—or to some people. But the world would be a sorry place without them. Anyone who hasn't any should at least borrow the friendship of a few—they're usually quite generous with that.

Who needs them? We all do!

The Way Easter Used to Be

April 11, 1974

One sounds like a real old-timer when harking back to the way things used to be in the good old days. Certainly not everything was better in the long-ago past, but it sure seems like the weather was! Not that we haven't had snow on Palm Sunday or Easter Sunday before, but way back when we were children, Easter was different. The most memorable custom was the Easter outfit. We always had an Easter outfit assembled during the annual, ritual shopping trip. You may have had to wear last year's spring coat, but you surely got a new straw hat and new shoes—usually black patent leather—and a pocketbook and (white!) gloves. And even a nice new pair of white socks.

In church on Easter Sunday morning, all the women and girls were resplendent. The boys had new suits, too (way back, of course, blue serge was the thing), and their fathers were sartorially splendid for the day. Everyone stood and chatted after church, and later the young people walked to the ice cream store for a sundae or ice cream soda, and a chance to see each other's Easter finery.

Easter outfits were the rule for kids and grandparents.

Brought up in this tradition, we continued it with our children. Every year there were the shopping trips and some of the chapeaux were memorable. There was one of natural straw that was bordered in field flowers, a white roller with navy streamers and one that was yellow and white straw with daisies on the grosgrain streamers that reminded me of something worn by the heroine of *Rebecca of Sunnybrook Farm*.

There also was the little white straw bonnet with the blue ribbons purchased one spring for the youngest of the family against her wishes. She just wanted no part of trying on hats. All the others, from the small son in his navy blazer and grey flannels through the girls, everyone had always had an Easter outfit. Perhaps this little one's rebellion was prophetic, because in this family, the Easter outfit long ago became a thing

Another Easter.

of the past. It has now become a source of harking back to the old days to look at the collection of snapshots of the annual lineup of the children in their Easter finery.

Last Easter Sunday there were some people dressed up for the joyful day, of course, but not the way they were in the old days when the clergyman in his pulpit looked out over a sea of colorful straw, ribbons, cherries and flowers. Perhaps this is all to the good if it means that churchgoers are paying more attention to Easter worship than to eyeing the costumes of their friends. On the other hand, dressing up was perhaps a very human outward sign of the joy of the occasion.

There will, however, be something traditional in the Roe Jan area this weekend besides the services in our many churches, including a sunrise service. That is the presentation at the Atheneum in Ancram of the old film, *Easter Parade*, featuring Irving Berlin's still popular song of the same name and starring Fred Astaire. It's rather nice this Easter, when the word "millinery" has apparently gone out of modern (American) English usage, to have something traditional like this still around.

And One to Go

September 19, 1974

Eight years ago this September was the first time a member of the family left home for college, and every couple of years thereafter, another set out for a college campus. In the meantime, there have also been those who have said their farewells and headed for an adventure and a temporary home in another country. Meanwhile, some have established homes of their own so, whether they visit for just a weekend or a summer, the time always comes when they must say goodbye.

That first time we delivered a college freshman to the opening day, we were surprised at the advanced age of some of the other freshmen's parents. Then it struck us that, by the time we delivered the last of six children to college fourteen years later, her roommate might suspect us of being her grandparents.

This year we took another freshman to college, one who jumped the gun by entering a year early, so we reached the point of "five down and one to go" sooner than we expected. By now, the trip to college had become an old

The grandsons, all grown up.

story to us as parents, and we no doubt appeared somewhat callous or blasé to the parents of the roommate who were leaving their first child there.

Worse yet was the first letter our poor college freshman received from home. Frustrated by the complete lack of time to write even one letter much less one to each of the four who were away at that point, I hastily typed a letter with carbon to all four, promising not to make it a habit. The fourth copy got caught in the typewriter, rolled itself around and became illegible. With not a moment to spare in which to type another, I quickly made a photocopy, put the four in the addressed envelopes at random and dashed off to the post office. As though a group letter and carbon copy were not bad enough, who should end up receiving the photocopy of a letter from home but the one who had just gone away for the first time! And I haven't even had time yet to write a personal note of apology for that wretched epistle that was scarcely any better than having to "read the paper if you want to hear from your mother," which I've been reminded of before.

Parents of just one child perhaps think it's hardest for them when that one goes, but that isn't altogether true. Although it's no doubt most quiet and lonesome when the last one, or the only one, leaves home, the parents—in fact, the remaining family—feels a wrench as each one goes. I can recall noticing when the children were all young that the atmosphere of the household changed even when any one of them was off visiting a schoolmate.

During the past couple of summers, so many of the younger members of the family have returned home for the vacation, and so many of their friends have come to visit that the household has resembled a youth hostel. This resulted, of course, in an endless round of meals to be cooked, dishes to be washed, groceries for which to shop and beds to make. But it also resulted in lots of fun, and our now shrunken household is very quiet by contrast. Except for weekends, when the nearest one and her friends descend upon us—like tomorrow! (We didn't stay lonesome for too long.)

Parents want their offspring to be able to go off into the world in high spirits, so we keep a fairly stiff upper lip for goodbyes. But as each one departs, it's as though a little something dies within us, perhaps no longer all whole because a part of us goes with them. Just the other day, when the one who was going to be away the farthest and longest was about to leave, I quite by chance came upon a motto that seemed extraordinarily appropriate: "there are only two lasting bequests we can give our children—one is roots, the other, wings."

The roots must be planted early and be strong from the very beginning in life. The wings must be encouraged to blossom and grow and take them out into the world where they can learn from it and give to it. And if those roots are good, healthy and strong, there need be no fear, even if absences are long, the winged creature will ever forget the way home.

An Exchange Mother

August 5, 1982

"You may never have been an exchange student, mom," I was told last week, "but you sure are an exchange mother!"

In 1967, when I succeeded in convincing several members of the community, after the departure of the first exchange student to live with our family, that it was a great experience and that we really should organize an exchange program, I had no idea that I would ever do more than act as a host mother to incoming students. We had just hosted

Having begun International Friendship Exchange, the community hosted many young exchange groups.

Rosmarie, a teenager from Chile, for two and a half months. When our new organization, International Friendship Exchange, received its first incoming group that summer, we hosted the leader, a young man of twenty-seven named Julio. As he hopped off the bus in Copake, he asked, "Are you my mother?" At that point, I wasn't old enough to be, but I shrugged and said yes, I guess so.

Subsequently, I became the mother of seventeen-year-old Kazue from Japan, twenty-four-year-old Annelies from Switzerland, twenty-year-old Maria Clara from Mexico and two other teenagers to whom my daughters had become sisters before I had the chance to play the role of their mother. Just a few weeks ago, I heard Norwegian Fride, now a young mother herself, calling me "Mommy" as she leaned across the table to attract my attention as we all visited in Bergen—her parents, her cousins, her aunt and uncle, and one of the babies who had come along to sleep through the party. Part of our trip was spent in the company of other Americans, and it was very enjoyable. But the most special part was the days we spent in the home of Fride's parents, who had been the parents of one of our daughters eleven years ago. We went to their home as she had, as people they'd never seen before. We shall never forget their hospitality, and that of the family with whom another daughter lived there.

Fride had come to us for a summer, as did Jill, the English sister of another of our own children. Meanwhile, we'd had the unique experience, just repeated in Norway, of meeting in Yorkshire her parents, the "parents" of one of our children. Later, in Switzerland, this experience was duplicated again, and we also spent time with our Swiss "daughter," who had lived with us through IFE. In fact, most of these wonderful experiences have been a result of friendships formed through IFE.

We are not the only family in this community to have had such great experiences resulting from involvement with our own local exchange program. Others have also had some of their exchange "children" return to visit again in their American homes. They have provided the home base for some of these young people from around the world when they have come to the United States to further their education. And some have even returned to bring their family's grandchildren!

Some of the young people participating in the IFE program this summer, those who went abroad as Community Ambassadors and those who have just arrived in the Roe Jan area from Germany, will enjoy the experience, benefit from it in many ways, but fail to continue the friendship that comes from it. But others will continue to keep in touch, perhaps they will return or they will welcome their host family to their own home for a future visit. In these cases the chains of friendship, once begun, will go on and on, forming a most wonderful bond between people—one that must be experienced to be totally understood. We come to truly love one another as real family and the dearest of friends.

IFE people can tell you about it, but you'll have to become one of them to really know it yourself.

CHAPTER 7
EVERYDAY THINGS

A GHOST WITH STICKY FINGERS

December 3, 1981

The subject of losing things happened to come up this week and someone said they most recently had lost something in their house. While this might seem like the easiest place to find the thing that was "lost," anyone who has had something vanish in their home knows better.

Perhaps, first of all, the word needs changing. What we can't find is not really lost, but rather, misplaced. Inanimate objects don't just disappear; someone has placed them somewhere in an unlikely spot. They will be discovered some day, perhaps when we move or by someone who comes after us, who will wonder why, for example, a pair of gloves is in a box of Christmas ornaments in the attic or a ring is sitting among paint cans in the cellar. There may have been a reason for them being left among unrelated objects, but we'll probably never remember what it was. The cause of said "losses" must be absent-mindedness. The gloves were protecting your hands from the needles of the discarded tree, perhaps, and the ring was taken off to avoid getting paint on it. Probably the phone rang as we set the gloves down for a moment or something distracted us, and the misplaced item was absent-mindedly left behind.

There is nothing more frustrating than one's inability to find such lost or misplaced things. One of their favorite hiding places is in a desk among hundreds of other papers. I once misplaced my Social Security card, and I went through desk drawers over and over, looking for it. I found lots of interesting letters from old friends, pictures the children drew when they were small and all sorts of memorabilia—but not the missing card. So, I had to apply to the Social Security office, and only when the missing one suddenly popped out of its hiding place years later did I realize its replacement was incorrect; it was a real problem in dealings with the IRS, but it no doubt was a good laugh for the ghosts or gremlins that keep these things hidden from our view.

It is so maddening, as you turn the house upside down searching for something, to know it is right there under your hand, while whatever it is that keeps things hidden taunts you—you ordinary mortal—who is incapable of seeing what's right before your eyes! This has happened so many times in our house over the years, and much more so recently, we have come to the conclusion that we must have a poltergeist. No, it doesn't bump things, not yet anyway; it just hides them (but it's a more interesting title than ghost).

It all began with the lace mitts that went with my wedding dress. The mitts had been in the box with it for thirty-four years until a daughter took the dress out for her wedding last winter. They were with the dress when she modeled it a few weeks before the wedding, but the next time the box was opened, they were gone. No—don't even suggest a place to look; we tried them all, ridiculous as some were. The mitts had simply vanished and were never seen again.

This reminded me of the sash to a favorite dress that had disappeared the previous summer, and the favorite yellow turtleneck someone else couldn't find. We began to put two and two together, coming up with the location of these three missing items. Just picture it. This little ghost is floating around here wearing a yellow turtleneck with a trailing green sash and the lace mitts.

But suddenly we realize that two and two made four after all, and this wraith's latest acquisition really has me worried. It's a backpack (a green one to match the sash nicely). Can't you see what's going to happen? That pack holds a lot, and I'm already missing a few more things I'll bet are stashed away in it.

Does anyone know how to find a poltergeist? That's something really difficult to put your hand on.

Another Kind of Bag Lady

November 18, 1982

School has now been in session forty days, according to my rough calculation—and I have not yet sent one lunch bag in that direction. When you consider that the basket on top of my refrigerator is presently overflowing with approximately seventy-eight prospective lunch bags, you must realize that my lunch bag surplus is reaching epidemic proportions. It was not always so.

Consider the fact that I first began accumulating and using small paper bags for this purpose 27 years ago (for the current, just grown-up generation, my mother collected them for me prior to that). You might have some notion of the number that passed through our kitchen and on to the school lunchroom over the years. Figure that the child who started school in 1953 and went to school about 180 days per year for 12 years (they don't carry lunch to half-day kindergarten) used that many lunch bags annually, totaling 1,260 bags by graduation (and, for a boy, the bags must increase in size each year). Formidable, isn't it?

Well, that's nothing. Now, multiple that number by six, and you'll see that this family went through 7,560 lunch bags in the course of its primary and secondary education, a fairly staggering statistic. Perhaps now you can understand the psychological implications of my present plight and the withdrawal symptoms of this kind of bag lady.

There was a time when I used to go out and buy a birthday card just to get another lunch bag when usage was at its height and the supply was running low. A greeting card bag is just the right size for one sandwich and a couple of nonbulky cookies. Those children who wanted two sandwiches and/or an apple had to have the kind of bag the storekeeper gives you with a very small purchase (the kind that might hold about five dollars' worth today). The bag that brought home a bottle of wine was fine for stacking up thick sandwiches and cookies with an apple in the bottom, but the self-conscious child who only took one sandwich cut them in half to disguise their original purpose so as to protect the family's reputation with the other kids at lunch.

Relatives and friends were helpful in those days. Compulsive bag smoothers, folders and savers that they were, they couldn't bear to discard a nice bag just fresh in from the store, but we were a good outlet and managed to use up their supplies as well as our own. Now, here I am in that same situation. (Have the psychologists studied this peculiar aspect of the empty-nest syndrome?) I carry my own lunch maybe once a week, so I should only save one small store bag each week. But once a saver, always a saver—I simply can't break the habit. And I have no relatives with school-age children needing lunch bags. There must be something else I can do with them. Perhaps I'll have to start a sideline in bag lunches to go, or I'll save them for the next paper bag shortage when I can make a tidy profit, black marketing lunch bags.

Then there's the time that I smuggled plastic bags home from Europe, but that's another story.

Old Memories and a New Year

January 13, 1983

One way of observing the rites of passage into the new year is by celebrating with frivolity on that final evening of the old year and making resolutions for improving one's life the first day of the new. Another way is to spend a quiet evening by the fire, reminiscing about the past year on December 31 and putting one's life in order for the coming year. And that has to include cleaning one's desk or closet, wherever one's most personal effects and memories are stored.

Going through the first drawer may be easy. The wastebasket is filled—and filled again—with all the really useless things that have been stored for future reference during the past year(s). There is an appalling statistic concerning the small percentage of things filed that are ever referred to again, and this could certainly apply as well to those things most of us don't actually file in any order but just stash away.

But then you reach the next drawer or shelf, and your perusal slows to a crawl as you begin to read cards, letters and other memorabilia. There are the programs of plays presented by the "baby" of the family ten years or so ago, poems written by the children when in grade school, loving messages on their homemade greeting cards that feature promises of breakfast in bed or lunch served on the patio. Then there are programs of their piano recitals, graduations and college baccalaureate ceremonies. A tiny envelope reveals the announcement of a child's birth, and a larger ivory one is the announcement of one's marriage.

There are letters from your own high school principal announcing an honor to be bestowed, from a dear friend who has since died, from your parents, from your children at camp, college or off on a foreign junket and from an author responding to your comments on her book. Anniversaries are relived through the many congratulatory cards saved. Journals recount the joys of a trip and the visits of exchange students. Brochures proclaim the beauties of places visited or still on the wish list.

With some resolve, a portion of this collection of memories may be pared down every few years. Someday, we realize, someone will have to toss it all out (unless they wish to write our biography). But for the moment, it makes good reading, and every life should have its history kept. We forget so much as time goes by that it's good to have these reminders.

When the new year dawns, we can again close the book on the past until its next reading, and we can get on with new plans, hang some new pictures, rearrange the furniture, start to read a new book and begin the first day of the rest of one's life.

A Place Shared

November 23, 1977

There is a place I like to go when I get the chance. It is a beautiful hilltop where one can look down on the valley or up still higher into the mountains. It's like being on top of the world, almost—like being of the world, but not in it. It doesn't belong to me, nor to anyone else who enjoys its beauty. But it beckons us, adult and child alike, to share its special magic.

The dog likes to go along. Nose to the ground, she scurries busily, to and fro. Many scents apparently lead nowhere, but suddenly she's onto something in the thicket that separates the hill from lower fields. As she dashes purposefully into the brush, a cock pheasant rises up squawking and flies off to the safety of another hiding place.

Now we start climbing toward the summit, up into the blue, blue sky of a wonderful day. From the top, one looks down on the village with a real bird's-eye view. To the north, there are rolling hills and the white church steeple in the next village. To the south, the beautiful farmland goes on and

Our beautiful countryside.

on, field after field and as far as the eye can see, separated by the now leafless hedgerows; the main highway is stretched across them like a ribbon, with lines of cars streaming up and down. Through the wooded area to the south, one looks down on the back of the village, an unfamiliar view, and the voices of children at play drift upward. One is high above the activity of the world, yet the traffic, even far below, is still a distraction.

Turning east toward the mountains and walking over the brink of the hill, suddenly all is silent; the sheltering hill blots out the sounds of the village and the highway below. Here, there are only the mountains and the sky. Smoke curling up from the chimney of one house on the hill is the only sign of life other than the busy exploration of the dog. Finally, even it disappears from view, and there is nothing to disturb the peace and quiet.

Suddenly, from the mountainside, two hawks appear; at first, only flashes of white make them visible as they fly. As they move out away from the mountain, they begin to soar in beautiful patterns as though their flight together were choreographed. They move rhythmically away from each other and then back again in circle after circle, swooping and passing, sometimes nearly meeting—or so it seems from far below. Finally the dance is over, and they fly apart; the first one disappears into the blue, and then the other.

The dog comes back, tired from her wandering, and flops down to rest—but not for long. She is soon her lively self again and decides it's high time this person played her game. One can ignore the dog for just so long. If she is to be satisfied, it's time to walk again, and it's time to relinquish the solitude of the hilltop and return to the workaday world and all its cares.

As we descend the hill, we hear a drone above; looking up, we see two small planes flying side by side, as though in imitation of the hawks but without the effortless and silent grace of the birds. Yet there must be a certain camaraderie in being able to leave earth behind and fly together, high above the rest of the world.

One must always come back to earth though, back down from the sky or from the hilltop. But for that little space in time there is the refreshment of soul of being removed from all else.

It isn't my hilltop, nor does it belong to any of the others who go there. But I am grateful to whoever shares it with us and lets us feel that we're welcome to walk there or to sit awhile, to escape from the world even while we have it spread before us in all its beauty.

CHAPTER 8

Public Affairs Near and Far

That Awful Moment

November 23, 1983

"I had never heard the word assassination before," recalls a woman who was a young child on this day twenty years ago. "But when our bus driver came into the schoolroom crying and said to our teacher, 'President Kennedy has been assassinated,' we knew what she meant. The teacher just said, 'Put on your hats and coats and go home, children,' and we all said a prayer on the way out of school."

Everyone remembers where they were and what they were doing at that moment when time seemed to stop. It was a day very much like this day twenty years later, even warmer. We were actually sitting out on the porch enjoying the lovely weather when we heard those terrible words. A chill came over the day.

Much has been written since that day about the terrible event that took place in Dallas. Surely it must have been seared on the memory of everyone who was there, who actually witnessed the horror of it. The horror, little diminished by distance, was shared over and over by all Americans, who were drawn to their television sets day after day that week and lived every moment with the family that shared its private tragedy with the whole world. And who can ever forget that incredible sight when, in the midst of on-the-spot news coverage, the accused assassin himself was murdered live on television.

Was that bright, sunny day in Dallas the beginning of a long string of such awful moments, assassination attempts—too many of them successful—that

Local graves of those who served.

have plagued those who dare to be leaders? And are we still as shocked as we were on that day, or has our shock level reached a point where we can accept such terrorism as simply part of life today?

This week we are deluged with perhaps more on the brief life of that young president than some even care to recall as the media dissects his aborted presidency. Was he a good president? Was he really the fine, idealistic hero people longed for? Was that "brief shining moment" really a touch of Camelot that went so fleetingly by that we hardly had a chance to experience it?

"I don't know," says this same young person who, even as a child, had glimpsed a vision of what this country—this world—might have become for her and her child. "He was my hero; I want to remember him that way."

And the memory of that sad and awful moment on November 22, 1963, lives on.

A Healing and a Memorial

November 18, 1982

Each year, as has been noted here before, the turnout of veterans for the local Memorial Day observance seems to grow smaller and older. A few veterans of service in the armed forces from the forties and fifties still don the uniform or the emblem of a veteran's organization, and they march down Main Street to lay a wreath at a monument to honor old men and women who have died in service to their country. But very few who served during the sixties and seventies join the march, although they have been urged by older veterans to do so in honor of their comrades who didn't come home.

A Memorial Day parade.

Who knows what has held these younger men and women back from joining in this public expression of caring that is so typical of small-town America? It might well have been the hurt they still held inside—the resentment and the wondering if their fellow Americans really cared that they had given those years out of their lives to fight a strange war in an alien country. They came home with scars, both physical and emotional, and certainly left behind the innocence and enthusiasm of youth with which they went. They returned, perhaps leaving part of themselves there emotionally, even physically, and certainly leaving behind many comrades who were missing in action as well as bringing home the bodies of those killed.

Many times in the years since Americans finally left Vietnam, it has been said by veterans of that war that they were never really welcomed home. Last week, many of them seemed to finally put those feelings of resentment and alienation to rest as they gathered in Washington for the five-day Salute to Vietnam Veterans and the official unveiling of the new stone memorial on the Mall that seems to be as controversial as the war whose participants it lists—all fifty-eight thousand of them. Some find it too grim, preferring a more traditional statue. But the U.S. involvement in Vietnam wasn't traditional; it was grim, and somehow the somber black wall with its simple listing of those incredible thousands of names, in the order in which they died, seems the most appropriate way to impress upon their fellow Americans the terrible enormity of this country's involvement and the awful sadness of the sacrifice of all those young Americans who never came home.

Some wondered why the television networks placed this story at the end of each night's news program instead of giving it first place. They were quite right in doing so, for how could viewers see who's talking about a football strike through misted eyes? Who, after watching men weep together, could care about Reagonomics?

Perhaps while veterans and spectators alike wept in Washington last week, Vietnam veterans and other Americans all over the country wept with them. Perhaps now, the tears have healed the hearts of all affected by that war. Perhaps next May, Vietnam veterans of the Roe Jan area will no longer be reluctant to be recognized and hopefully will want to join in the annual memorial with and for their neighbors.

Public Servants—What Makes Them Run?

October 24, 1974

During the past week, two new political clubs have been formed, with their main purpose, of course, being to get their candidates elected. During the previous weekend, one of the older clubs had a Meet Your Candidates Night, introducing several men aspiring to hold public office. A week ago today, a man who is determined to unseat a longtime incumbent dashed around the Roe Jan area all afternoon in an effort to meet the voters after having spent the earlier hours of that day making the same earnest effort elsewhere. And tonight there will no doubt be more such aspirants eating turkey at the umpteenth supper they've attended in the past month while talking a little turkey with the voting public there.

One might ask, in the face of all this frenetic activity, which happens every autumn all over the United States, why? Why does anyone in their right mind want to undergo the rigors of the campaign trail, much less the responsibility that follows if one is successful in being elected? Do they forget, in the excitement of the campaign, the loneliness of the job they so

When the congressman comes, *right*, he finds the town supervisor on his farm.

Local supervisors talk politics beside the milk tanker.

eagerly seek; or the loneliness caused by the peculiarity of human beings that causes them to abandon their faith in anyone who is elected to public office or any other kind of representation of the people? Are they able to overlook, in their shining hour of triumph on election night, the stark fact that, especially if the office is the one at the top of whatever structure of government, town or nation, it is the lonely place where, as Harry Truman said, "the buck stops here"?

The rest of us ordinary citizens are fortunate that there are talented, responsible and qualified men and women who can overlook all the drawbacks in the life of a public servant. It is unfortunate, however, that we tend to overlook the fact that this is just what they are willing to make of themselves—servants of the public.

Just as a certain mistrust of anyone holding an elective post is a peculiarity of the electorate, another peculiar quirk of human nature is the suspicion that everyone else has a soft job. This belief is all too often applied in assessing the responsibilities of our town officials, for example. The salaries, if looked at in the light of present standards, are obviously only for part-time work. Yet the workload of some of these offices has tripled in recent times.

The average voter, pulling down the lever for the candidate of his choice, scarcely has any notion just what duties that office entails. In the case of any town official, it may be assumed that, if elected, he or she will simply attend the monthly meeting of the town board. Who knows anything of the countless hours many officials put into their part-time jobs every month?

A justice, for example, has to be at court a certain night each week, whether any cases appear, and for many hours when they do. Since the State Magistrate's Association frowns on "court in the kitchen," he is expected to drive to the town office at any time—day or night—that the police bring someone to him.

The assessors meet every month, although not required to, in order to keep up with laws affecting the assessment of property and recent sales of parcels within the town. Their chairman works extra hours to check records at the courthouse and to assist people with forms. The tax collector also goes beyond required duties in helping people with forms and works over a holiday, while others make merry, in order to get tax bills out early enough to give taxpayers plenty of time to pay before penalties would be imposed.

The clerk's job is, of course, extremely demanding with a tremendous amount of paperwork and filing, to say nothing of being at the beck and call of the public at all hours. Furthermore, in the case of the clerk, the collector and the supervisor, the official's home becomes his office, and a great deal of one's privacy is thus sacrificed. The premises are used by townspeople for official business although no rent is paid for them by the town.

The highway superintendent's job is also one of the most demanding in a town. He must be on call twenty-four hours a day and, often when storms make roads impassable, he performs acts of kindness to townspeople far beyond the normal call of duty.

Even the town historians, who receive a negligible salary for what had been a small job, are now doing much extra work in response to requests, for family histories and other such information, for which no fees are paid.

The man at the top, of course, is the one who, perhaps because of the title of the post, seems to be the one town figure responsible for every detail of town affairs. At least it seems that way when his phone rings day and night and in the wee hours of the morning, with requests to solve every kind of problem. Basically, the supervisor's job is to be not only fiscal officer of the town, but he is also a member of his town board and of the county board of supervisors. The latter is a post with responsibilities that grow ever more demanding with membership on county committees and also more grave, as in the case of that governing body being called upon to make a decision for or against nuclear power.

If any of the local elective offices could be called a full-time job, the supervisor's certainly should. Yet somehow the men who fill this lonely spot at the top in each of our towns in the Roe Jan area also manage to operate their own business, and some are even involved in other volunteer community efforts. There just aren't enough hours in anyone's day for this much work, and something has to give somewhere. Something gets cheated of time, and unfortunately it's most apt to be the family. Anyone involved in public services, whether in office or strictly as a volunteer, is stealing the time for it from their personal life.

How many people who have the qualifications to do a good job will continue to willingly make these sacrifices, not only in time but in money? Not only are the officials' salaries modest, the six hundred dollars allotted a supervisor for bookkeeping expenses, secretarial help and someone to answer phone calls around the clock is incredible. Yet in addition to his services, the town official gives the public the use of his home, his telephone and his automobile (with countless calls and miles thrown in at no charge to the taxpayer).

What makes anyone run for office? Political reasons perhaps, but as one energetic candidate stated here recently, "Once elected you serve all the people." We're fortunate in the Roe Jan area to have so many dedicated citizens serving us so well.

TV on Cold Water Street

March 28, 1974

There seems to be no end to the variety of activities that take place in the life of this small rural community. But what happened on Cold Water Street in Hillsdale Saturday afternoon tops them all—at least for the moment.

Who would have ever expected to drive down that rather narrow residential street in their reasonably quiet country village of an afternoon and see a big, hand-lettered banner stretched across the front entrance of a fine Colonial house reading Colgan for Congress? One side of the street was lined with cars, a few children stood looking at the house (and, most likely, a few neighbors peered out their front windows to see what was going on), but otherwise no one would suspect that an auspicious event was taking place within that venerable old home.

But at that moment, a television camera was grinding away to record the moment when a virtually unknown young man—not a familiar figure even in his own community—was announcing to all who listened there (and all the thousands or millions who would view the brief segment on the six o'clock newscast) that he was intending to run for a seat in Congress next November.

It was as simple as that. Bill Colgan—a social studies teacher who was still in his twenties, married and the father of one child, a householder on Cold Water Street (his neighbor was hosting this unusual gathering)—had made up his mind that he was going to become a member of the House of Representatives or at least prove that it's still possible for an ordinary citizen to run for office in America. One wondered, listening, what other such momentous events might have taken place within those old walls.

Bill has no wealth and no wealthy friends who would gladly buy him that seat in the House in return for a favor. And if he did—and they tried—it was very evident they'd be turned down flat. Bill Colgan is his own man in that respect, but he wants to be a true man of the people if he gets to those hallowed halls of the Capitol. He said it plain and well last Saturday: "I want to make the word 'representative' ring true."

This may not be the first time the hamlet of Hillsdale has been on television, and in these days of super communication, it probably won't be the last, but it certainly doesn't happen every day on Cold Water Street. How very fine it was that, when the TV camera came to town it was to record not a disaster or some other dreadful event, but the historic moment when a forthright young man pledged himself to represent his fellows.

We were glad to be there.

The First Beautiful Step

June 17, 1982

> *How beautiful on the mountains are the feet of one who brings good news, who heralds peace.*
> *—Isaiah 52:7*

How beautiful, upon the avenues of that great city, must have been the march of those thousands of feet, of the thousands of people of all ages, races, religions and nationalities who joined in one cause last Saturday in New York to bring good tidings and preach peace.

Surely they do not all see the means to peace in the same way. Some demand unilateral disarmament; others do not. Some oppose the armed forces; others gladly served in them. What they do agree on is a desire to "choose life" over death and to achieve the peaceful world that was surely meant to be. As one who was there on June 12 says, the majority of peace seekers may have been quite unsophisticated and naïve. They don't have all the answers—many probably don't understand the precautions that the more conservative feel must be taken.

But what they are suggesting is that someone has to take the first step. In any conflict of ideas, beliefs and ideologies, someone has to offer compromise; someone has to give a little. And last Saturday, 500,000 people of mixed persuasions and backgrounds stuck their necks out, put their best foot forward and proclaimed to their governments that they yearn for peace.

"Behold the turtle, who makes progress only when he sticks his neck out."

Governments, large and small, must now heed the good news, the cry for peace brought to them by their people. It is now up to governments to decide how it can become a reality, to stick their necks out to achieve it. It has begun in such a typically American way, at the grass roots of small towns, where people have voted in town meetings in favor of seeking a nuclear freeze. In New England states, all the citizens vote at town meetings. Here in New York, members of elected boards are being asked to resolve that something be done toward achieving peace. It will take courage on the part of these local representatives to do so, but they must find a way. They need not endorse a public petition per se if it doesn't express their particular views. Instead, they might word their own resolution in support of peace in whatever way they believe it can be realized.

And then some day, the children, grandchildren or great-grandchildren of the youngsters who led the June 12 march—or maybe even those children themselves—can say "now we finally have a world at peace, and the day it began, I was there."

CHAPTER 9

On Language

Podium, Podia or Lectern?

October 8, 2009

William Safire has died. Conservative readers of his political column in the *New York Times* will miss him; liberals will not, even if they had to admire his wit. In an announcement of his death, Times Co. chairman Arthur Sulzberger Jr. noted his "insightful political commentary" and his "wonderful sermons on the use and abuse of language." As another report on his death noted, "he pontificated with wit and erudition about the corruption of language in American politics and journalism."

It was that which made me a fan of his Sunday *Times* column, "On Language." In fact, while searching old files of correspondence, I find a postcard response to something I had written to him in 1986 about language. It reads, "I'm grateful for your comments on the column. English expects all of us to do our duty." Strangely, in that very extensive file, usually containing both a letter and response, I now know not what prompted me to write.

For years, it seems, I have been indignant about a misuse of the word podium (plural podia), which keeps getting worse and worse! Yet I never corresponded with him on that, unfortunately, and I don't know whether he ever wrote about it in his column. Google gives a simple definition and even states that "the noun podium has one sense: a platform raised above the surrounding level to give prominence to the person on it." Oxford American Dictionary goes further to say that a podium is "a small platform on which a person stands to give a speech or conduct an orchestra." Merriam Webster concurs; the main purpose of the platform is for an orchestra conductor's use. It is interesting to note that these are recent editions, up to 2008, not bending to popular (incorrect) usage and meaning of the word podium.

Yet, everyone in America, from the president on down, keeps talking and writing about being "at the podium." That gives visions of being down on the floor, since a conductor's podium seems to be hardly a foot high. Part of the problem is that what they really refer to is a lectern, which Google gives again: "one sense: desk or stand with a slanted top used to hold a text at the proper height for a lecturer." The roots of these two confused nouns should give a clue to their meaning and use: "lect" as in lecture, having to do with speaking; "pod" as in, for example, podiatry, having to do with the foot, thus a platform on which to stand, while speaking of material placed on a lectern.

All of which make me sound as much a curmudgeon as Safire. Well, others will continue to write columns expounding on their particular political views. But who will protect the language? We all should do our duty.

Try This on for Size

August 6, 1981

What strange things the business community is doing to the language these days! Has it always been thus? My father was a businessman but I don't recall hearing him speak jargon. Today, however, every business has its own language, not only the strictly technical language but also some vocabulary that spills over into the vernacular of the general public. How many people recognized the meaning of words like "perks" a year ago, except when it referred to something coffee does while brewing?

Just once, several years ago, I used in these pages a jargon word that has become common enough to be included in the *American Heritage Dictionary*, although the Usage Panel deplores it and says so immediately below its definition. It is the word that ads for that fine dictionary tell us that Edwin Newman—surely one of the most erudite persons seen and heard on TV—abhors. "Finalizing a schedule?" the ad asks. "Edwin Newman isn't." The copy goes on to say that 90 percent of the panel, which advises the publisher, believe "anything can be completed or put in final form without resorting to bureaucratic jargon such as *finalize*." And when I used it, echoing some news source who had used it on me, Jim Carlson chided me immediately on my poor usage, and I didn't blame him.

But such purists had better brace themselves for a whole new spate of words with that *–ize* suffix that will probably appear in the dictionaries before long. Here is a warning list garnered from the mail crossing my desk:

(1) In order to dispose of garbage in the future, environmentalists have gone the lexicographers one better. The refuse will not just be pelleted (which appears in the dictionary) but *pelletized.*

(2) A shirt is advertised as being *qualitized.* Does the Better Business Bureau know what this means?

(3) For years, the local board of education has been saying it must get down to its "goals and priorities." Another local group gets to the point much quicker, merely stating it is about to *prioritize.*

(4) A release from the government tells how it has *incentivized*, which sounds like a euphemism for the slangier, but sometimes serious, "brainwashing."

(5) A religious group predicts that religion will become *privatized* (Did the holy hermits of yore realize that they started it?)

(6) Of course, a consumer can not only have an article personalized, a good old word with proper credentials, but the *–ize* craze has spawned endless *–ize* things that can only improve the quality of life while putting a trade name on the tip of the public tongue. For example, *Midasize.*

Then of course, one can have more fun by taking some acceptable old *–ize* words and prefixing them with *de-*, which indicated a removal from whatever the word means. I'd always thought airline stewardesses made up the word deplane to put themselves on a plane with ship's stewards who debark. Maybe they did, but the dictionary defines it. And while I understand "briefing," "debriefing" has always seemed a funny word. I don't know if it gives the rather somber Ed Newman a chuckle, but I picture the debriefed as being totally denuded of whatever information lurked in their brains, poor things. And just picture being "dehypnotized." Talk about being completely undone!

But now that we've institutionalized certain kinds of individuals, the mail tells us that they are now being *deinstitutionalized.* And the nuclear energy people report that things are being *denormalized.* The trouble is I don't remember whether the ones who wrote that were for or against.

I hope you'll notice that I have particularized the foregoing words for you, particularizer that I am, which brings us to legalese. But if we don't even understand the *-ize* vocabulary yet, we'd better shy away from that which makes businessese look like child's play.

To finalize, let's just get incentivized to prioritize whether to pelletize, qualitize, privatize or simply Midasize.

Epilogue

A Hometown to be Thankful For

November 21, 1973

The fact that our "hometown"—not just our particular township or village, but the whole Roe Jan area—is set in beautiful country is certainly obvious to the most casual motorist passing through. It's apparently obvious to those who hurry back to the lakes each summer and the slopes each winter, with many making the pilgrimage every weekend.

It should follow that it is perfectly obvious to all of us who live here all year-round, although unfortunately there are those who fail to see what is right under their noses. But living each day amid such beautiful country is indeed something to be thankful for.

However, there are more than just the physical surroundings to be grateful for when one lives in the country. The community spirit and the many activities that people become involved in are perhaps unique to rural or "small-town" life. The very nature of some of our activities is foreign to a city dweller.

Recently, I was discussing with some people visiting here from enormous cities the Corn Day I had just photographed, and one, a photographer himself, asked what a Corn Day is. I explained it as a demonstration (of experimental plantings, etc.), and this amused him and yet struck him as rather wonderful.

"Where I live," he said, "A demonstration is when crowds of people are in the street throwing things at policemen."

Sally gives awards at a Ramble.

But there is still something else that is my favorite of all things about living here. It's a small thing and may sound silly, yet it's quite astonishing to city visitors. That is, that as I drive up and down Route 22 or almost anywhere in the Roe Jan area, each day the people I pass in every few cars coming toward me wave at me, and I wave back. And when I go in and out of the store and post office, for example, people know me and greet me. I find myself smiling happily, for I think this is positively wonderful. Just compare this with a day spent in the city or a large town where, if you go about alone, perhaps no one—absolutely no one—speaks to you all day long.

Now, as much as this business of practically everyone knowing each other amazes city folk, it also appalls many of them. Having become accustomed to anonymity, they don't think they like the idea of "everyone knowing all about you."

Well, first of all, no one ever really knows all about you, unless you tell it all. But if and when you meet someone in your daily rounds and they ask you questions about yourself and your family, you can make a judgment on this, if you'd like.

Are they just being nosey or is it because they care about me?

I prefer to believe it is the latter. And I am thankful for their caring.

A Small Town

November 18, 1976

A small town is where:

Your grown-up cousin, or even your mother, drives the school bus.

When you dial a wrong number, you recognize the voice that answers and get into a conversation.

A local official knows everyone by name; and if he doesn't, he can refer you to his mother who will.

You can stand in the middle of the street talking to a friend all day and not get run over.

If someone, even from out of town, calls the telephone company to report that your home phone out of order, they'll offer to connect them with your office or wherever they expect you'd be at the moment.

You not only can name everyone on your street but maybe almost everyone in your whole village.

Everywhere you go about your daily business—the gas station, the store, the post office or the bank—everyone knows your name.

The original general store and church.

Chris, a young patriot.

When you spy someone walking down your road, you question who it is, as though you should know everyone who walks on the street where you live.

Someone can send you a letter without a street address—or even your full name—and you'll get it.

If you drop a letter at the post office without postage or the proper address, it won't go to the dead-letter office; it will reappear in your box, or there will be a note saying you owe postage for the letter that was already sent on its way.

When you're in the hospital, one hundred people know about it and send you a card.

When you stop at the drive-in window of the local bank, you not only get a pleasant greeting through the microphone, but a little chat about whatever might be happening in your family at the moment.

When you read someone's name in the local paper, you actually know who they are, and so does the editor.

The city is a great place to visit, as they say, but isn't it fun to live in a small town?

"Doc" Mettler's Stories

"Down Maple Lane" sometimes had contributions from other members of the family who worked on the *Independent* from time to time. A collection of those written by the father of the family was compiled after his death and these are a few favorites.

On Christmas Eve, in a Stable

By John J. Mettler Jr., DVM

How the Beasts Keep Christmas
By Phyllis McGinley

At midnight's stroke,
In barn, in stall,
Kneel all
The dumb folk.

Meekly bow
In reverence, then,
The silly hen
The horned cow,

For a breath's space.
And ass and ox

Makes, each, his box
A kneeling place.

Even the dark
Forest peoples
Hear the steeple's
"Hark! Hark!"

And glory wheels
Through den and lair.
Besides the hare
Fox kneels,

Till all on earth
Of fur or feather
Praise together
Christ's birth,

The when or why
Can none recall,
Yet kneel all.
And kneel I.

The only sound is the snow crunching under your boots. When it makes that sound, you know it is close to zero. Most times you think of December nights as pitch-black and not too cold, but tonight, with almost a full moon, it is bright and cold. The track on the barn door makes a squeak as you open it, not because it needs oil but because it too is cold. I wonder how cold it was in Bethlehem that night.

Even before you snap on the lights, something, maybe just the "feel" of the air—sort of a sixth sense—will tell you if something is wrong. That something could be a loose calf, a cow down or a leaking water bucket. There wasn't any water in that stable in Bethlehem that night. They sent a young boy for hot water, but he never did come back.

The smell of clean cattle, along with hay and straw, gives a farmer a sense of security that is hard to describe. Is this feeling a memory from boyhood when you went to the stables after supper with your father? Or does it go back further into the heritage of all of us, whose lifework involves cattle, back to how Joseph must have felt as he finally found a warm, dry place for his beloved Mary?

Dr. Mettler speaks at the historical society.

After you snap on the light, you listen. Cattle and sheep all cough from time to time but too much coughing, or too much silence, is cause for alarm. This night, this holy night, the only sound is the normal peaceful swish and low rumble of cows eating hay. If a stranger came in, the sound would stop. I wonder if it was all silent that night as it says in the song.

The first thing you look at is the cow in the box stall, now a week overdue to calve. She lies there, chewing her cud. You think of the song again, "all is calm, all is bright." What could be more calm than a cow chewing her cud?

You fluff the bedding and push the hay up in the mangers. There is no need to do this in modern barns, but this is the only time of day you can be alone with your cows and your thoughts.

Something touches your leg. It is one of the barn cats rubbing against you. I wonder if there were any small animals in the stable that night. A stable wouldn't be a stable without a cat.

One last look around: Old Effie in the box stall won't calve tonight yet, so you can go to sleep without a worry. Nothing unusual tonight—just a routine bedtime check. And yet, it is the anniversary of that special night.

You step out into the cold again. To the north, the aurora borealis is sending up fireworks, and to the south, your neighbor's Christmas lights twinkle like the stars. Yes, just another night—I wonder if that's the way it seemed in Bethlehem that night.

A Special Kind of Person

By John J. Mettler Jr., DVM

At 4:35 a.m. on a Christmas morning, I pulled out of Maple Lane and headed north on Route 22. Snow had been falling since midnight, and there were no fresh tracks until I reached the upper exit of Copake Falls. There I could see human footprints in the glow of the headlights. A mile further on, I spotted a figure walking rapidly, hunched into the wind. I stopped and he got in.

"Where you going?"

"Hillsdale to the tank yard; got to leave by five o'clock to pick up across the river and couldn't get my car started. Sure glad you came along."

Here was a young man who had gotten out of bed at 4:00 a.m. on a Christmas morning to leave his wife and young children to do a difficult, often dangerous and unpleasant job for the next twelve hours: picking up milk from the farms. I say twelve hours—the normal run is supposed to take eight hours or less. But like the traditional mailman of old, neither sleet, rain, flood, mud or snow can be allowed to stop the milk tanker driver from his rounds, whether it takes six hours or twenty-four.

The milk pickup truck drivers are a new breed of men. They must be able to negotiate the narrowest, most crooked country lane and the busiest city street. They also have to be trained and talented enough to check the milk in a farm bulk tank by appearance and odor. They must also take sterile samples from the tank for later checking for bacteria, flavor, antibiotics or other contaminants at the milk plant.

They have to be able to drive the most difficult type of load. A partially loaded tanker will flip over like a canoe if there is a sudden swerve of the wheels or application of the brakes. Besides this, each driver must be a public relations man, having the confidence of both the dairy farmer—that he is measuring the milk accurately—and also the plant manager, to whom he must deliver the correct number of pounds.

Most of us have high regard for truckers, as men who are proud to be doing a good job. But I can't say enough in praise of the milk truck pickup driver. Last week, one young driver nearly sacrificed his own life to avoid hitting a car that rounded a curve on a county highway in the middle of the road. He knew that to take to the ditch with a partial tank of milk to avoid the oncoming car made his own crash certain. But he didn't hesitate because, like most truckers, he didn't want to hurt anyone else.

It is good to know there are still men of his character around, working not just for the money but because there is a job to be done.

The Call of the Wild Goose

By John J. Mettler Jr., DVM

At first glance it was just another flock of geese going north, but something was different. The sky was the blue that only a cloudless April day can make it, and the sun, up only a few minutes, shone from behind the ridge, making everything sparkle. I stood and stared, as I always do at geese, but what was different?

The classic *V* formation was more like a great wide *U*, and the ends undulated like a slack fish line might over the ripples in a stream. Were they ducks? No—too big for ducks, and it had at least eighty in line.

Having just stepped out of the darkness of the barn, it took my eyes a second or two to adjust to the light, and then I could see the snow-white breasts and the shiny black wing feathers: snow geese!

I call the other men from the barn. "Come here; have you ever seen snow geese before?" The four of us stood in awed silence, each of us sure we had never seen anything like it before. The only way to describe the great birds was to say they were like some artist's conception of an angel. We watched them until they were out of sight beyond the ridge that marks the north end of the Harlem Valley.

Yes, they were snow geese, but all day something bothered me. Beautiful as they were, and as pleased as I was at having seen them, there was something missing.

Late that evening, when I was miles away from home, I looked up at the sky and, by instinct, stood and listened. Suddenly I knew the answer: those snow geese flew in complete silence. Then and only then did I realize that no matter how beautiful the snow geese were, it was the absence of the lonesome and disturbing call that first made me know they were different.

The call of the Canada goose probably doesn't affect everyone the way it does me, although I know it gives many people the same thrill. I think I inherited the feeling from my father. When we were kids on the farm in North Hillsdale, wild geese were rare compared to today. In the spring or fall, if my father heard a flock going over while on his barn check, he would come running into the house, calling, "come out, quick! The geese are flying."

We'd run out and stand there shivering in the cold, waiting for a glimpse of the geese against the moon. Often, all we would see was a dark sky and Dad standing there with the lantern as he listened. He never had but a third-grade education, but he wanted his children to learn all they could both in and out of school. The call of the geese was only part of the story. Where they had been, where they were going, how they mated for life, how loyal they were and how smart—all of these things a young person should learn.

The silence of the snow geese made me realize what I must have really known all my life, that it is the sound more than the sight of the geese that matters most.

The call of the wild Canada goose has had a great effect on my life. It is a disturbing, yet fascinating sound. To hear it and not be able to heed it is the worst thing.

This is the way it affected my father. He wanted to learn what was far to the north and, in all other directions, what was beyond the farthest hill. He loved his valley and didn't ever want to leave it for long, yet deep inside he had the curiosity that prompts men to want to learn what is on the other side of the ridge.

To follow the lonesome call of the wild goose is not a "wild goose chase," because the goose always comes back. He leaves in sadness—his call sounds it—and yet he always returns.

About the Author

Elinor Mettler started her writing career covering fashion for a magazine of the shoe industry in New York City. In 1947, she married veterinarian Dr. John J. Mettler Jr. and moved to the upper Hudson Valley. There, she raised six children and founded the Roe Jan *Independent*, a weekly newspaper serving five towns. She edited and published the *Independent* for thirteen years. Mrs. Mettler was also active in the community. She founded the Roeliff Jansen Historical Society, serving as president and organizing exhibits. She was instigator of the Harlem Valley Rail Trail; served as trustee at a local hospital; founded the International Friendship Exchange, a foreign exchange program for local students; and also founded the Roe Jan Ramble, an annual road race through the area. In 2000, the New York Parks and Conservation Association granted her the Greenway and Community Trail Spark Plug Award, recognizing her commitment and achievement in developing and promoting greenways and community trails. In 2009, Mrs. Mettler was named Copake Community Day Grand Marshal, in honor of her long-standing community leadership. Previous publications include *The Fagan Sisters: A History of Life in a New York Country Village* (Arcadia) and *Love Always*, a collection of World War II letters (self-published). She also created two films about agriculture in the area and recorded oral histories of old-time local residents.